The Church That Could Be

David Edwards was a Fellow of All Souls College, Oxford, from 1952 to 1959, and became a priest in the Church of England in 1955. He was Editor and Managing Director of SCM Press from 1959 to 1966 and also an honorary curate at St Martin-in-the-Fields, before a time in Cambridge as Dean of King's College. From 1970 to 1978 he was a canon of Westminster Abbey, serving also as Rector of St Margaret's, the Speaker's Chaplain in the House of Commons and Chairman of Christian Aid. From 1978 to 1994 his main work lay in cathedrals, as Dean of Norwich and Provost of Southwark. He has also written many books, mainly historical, and been involved with journalism, mainly at the *Church Times*, and has been awarded a Lambeth Doctorate of Divinity and an OBE. He now lives in Winchester and assists in the cathedral there.

The Church That Could Be

DAVID L. EDWARDS

Published in Great Britain in 2002 by
Society for Promoting Christian Knowledge
Holy Trinity Church
Marylebone Road
London NW1 4DU

British Library Cataloguing-in-Publication Data
A catalogue record for this book is available from the British Library

ISBN 0-281-05455-X

Designed and typeset by Kenneth Burnley, Wirral, Cheshire
Printed in Great Britain by The Bath Press–CPI Bath

Contents

Preface

I KNOW THAT THIS BOOK was written with passion but I hope that it is also sensible. It is based on the experiences of a life beginning in 1929 but it is also a piece of thinking because I have used what I have learned in order to make suggestions intended to be forward looking. They are suggestions about Christianity, for I have been fascinated by its past and its present, and seriously worried – but also ultimately hopeful – about its future. I have referred to some books, including some of my own, and that may suggest some further reading; but I hope that this summary of a long education in subjects which are not small has the merits of simplicity and brevity. Of course it leaves a lot out, including almost all events outside Britain until the last chapter.

In particular I thank Ruth McCurry, publisher and friend, who saved me from making the book even more passionate and personal than it still is. Even now the frequency of 'I' needs forgiveness.

It is not a 'how-to-fill-your-church' kind of book, nor does it advise you how to build your own new church inside you – indeed it is not very like any other book known to me – but it tries to look at the Christian Church as the conveyor of a message and to confront the fact that at present most people in Britain and the rest of Europe think that the message is untrue and unconnected with what matters.

I therefore dedicate this very personal book to all who survive after helping me on my way; to friends who do more than survive, having died; and to those who will have to make the changes needed in the Christian Church, whether or not they agree with my own views and whether or not they notice my absence.

DAVID L. EDWARDS

CHAPTER 1

Two Worlds

M Y LIFE HAS TAKEN ME into two worlds which can seem out of contact with each other – the traditional world of the churches and the world of modern knowledge and life. And in my experience one of these worlds has been successful.

Over the 45 years while I have been a priest of the Church of England its active membership has been reduced by about a half. Large numbers have remained semi-attached, as well-wishers and occasional attenders, with or without orthodox beliefs, but this constituency also seems likely to diminish. Only a quarter of the nation's marriages is now solemnized in the Church of England and less than a quarter of the babies is brought to it for baptism; in the 1950s it baptized about two-thirds.

The number of baptized Roman Catholics in Britain increased from about 2 million to about 5 million during the twentieth century, largely thanks to immigration and a comparatively high birth rate, but the number attending Mass was approximately the same when the century ended as when it began. In other words, most dropped out.

The active membership of the Church of Scotland declined by a third during the century, in a population which grew by more than a tenth. In the same period the decline of Nonconformity in Wales was even more severe, and the Anglican and Roman Catholic statistics, although better, were no compensation. In Britain's Protestant and Free churches losses by the Methodists and the United Reformed Church have been balanced by Baptist steadiness and by gains in the Pentecostal and Independent churches, but the only churches to experience impressive growth have been the congregations of the Black British, which have been social clubs as well as spiritual homes valued in a chilling environment.

Obviously such statistics set the alarm bells ringing and the sound has certainly been heard in Britain's churches – but a softer sound is harder to hear: it is a time-bomb ticking. In many periods there have been among the churchgoers more old than young, and more women than men, but the absence of the young and the men became more than usually dangerous during the last century. The extent of the danger has been partly concealed by the obstinate faithfulness of the elderly, but this age group to which I belong is not immortal. Another problem is that the oldies are already creating a financial crisis because of the need to pay pensions to clergy and widows; in the Church of England, such pensioners are now approximately equal in number to the salaried clergy.

In all the churches life and faith have become more organized during this period of contraction. Of course something like this tends to occur in any shrinking organization which seems fated to think that it must make further contraction likely by becoming absorbed in time-consuming problems of finance and reorganization. However, if one views the churches from the inside, or perhaps as a sympathetic outsider, one can see that as the surrounding society has become more secular, the churches have become more religious. When churchgoing cannot be regarded as fashionable or conventional, people who do go listen more, participate more, give more and receive more. They believe in a more heartfelt way, belief being now more often a conscious decision to trust in the God of salvation rather than in respectable customs; and what they believe has a distinguishable effect on how they behave. A 'faith community' (a new term) becomes a sub-culture and in its ethos a counter-culture. Here important memories are stored, significant relationships are made, the faith is a point from which a world is viewed, and this world may look very different from what is seen from other points, particularly if in another worldview the horizon is not eternity. Any depression caused by the declining statistics may be soothed by confident talk which can seem credible when the members of this minority talk mostly with each other. Yet this confidence may not halt the statistical decline. If enquirers are told the terms of admission without concessions (as when a mother wants her baby to be baptized because she wants 'the best for the baby' and she is met with an alarming list of the religious commitments needed), they may be glad that they have found what they were looking for – but they are more likely to read their reception as a No Entry sign. It seems that in order to grow, the churches need a kind of confidence which is not repulsive.

This decline in churchgoing has been in part caused by, and in part a cause of, the decline in Christian beliefs. Surveys of public opinion have suggested that about a quarter of the population now definitely disbelieves in the existence of God, or at least is sure that we have no means of knowing anything about this subject; in the 1950s the proportion was no more than a tenth. The rest do not wish to call themselves atheists or complete agnostics, but now the majority of those who tell pollsters that they 'believe in God' believes in a 'higher power' or 'life force', not in 'a God who concerns himself personally with every human being' and is at least 'personal'. Almost half are reported to believe that Jesus was 'just a man', and about half that there can be no life after death. Although a MORI poll in 1993 suggested that the majority of those who go to church every week believes that 'the Bible is God's word and every word in it is true', the overwhelming majority of those who are not such frequent attenders puts the beliefs that Jesus was born of a virgin and rose physically from his tomb among the Bible's legends. Although the majority of frequent churchgoers disapproves of sex before marriage and (more strongly) of 'practising' homosexuality, the majority within this majority is of an age when interest in sex of any kind has passed its peak. Among people for whom that is not true, the only forms of sexual activity which are commonly thought to be clearly wrong are adultery (except that not many are surprised) and, for the unmarried, intercourse outside a relationship which both partners can call love. And this seems to be the sexual morality practised by many of those among the young who definitely regard themselves as Christians. According to the estimate in *British Social Attitudes 2001–2* 55 per cent of the population of Britain would like to be counted as 'Christian' and only 5 per cent as belonging to 'other faiths', but the reality seems to be that if 'Christian' is defined in a strictly traditional sense, the 40 per cent said to have 'no religion' must be doubled.

*　　　　*　　　　*

In the rest of Europe the situation seems to be much the same. It is estimated that in this continent which used to be Christendom, with a much frequented church dominating both the appearance and the life of almost every village or town, at least a third of the population is now thoroughly secular, while for another third any link with a church is feeble. In France, which used to be called the Eldest Daughter of the Church (under a king officially called Most Christian), the secular state now provides no religious education in the schools which it controls, and the Catholic Church cannot fully provide the sacraments in the parishes because it cannot recruit enough priests: the number of parish priests was halved in the 30 years after 1965, leaving half of those left over 60 years old. Across Europe religious beliefs are wider than regular church attendance; only in Sweden do fewer than half the people tell pollsters that they believe in 'God'. But many popular beliefs – in horoscopes, for example, or in Fate – would be called superstitious by the churches, and if the unorthodox end up in hell three quarters of present-day Europeans will be surprised to find that it exists.

If we ask why Europe has become the scene of a disaster on this scale for its churches, a part of the answer is that they abused what used to be their great power. Their abuse of an official monopoly in the sphere of religion was not confined to notorious cases of cruel persecution by the medieval Inquisition which tortured and burned 'heretics' or by Byzantine emperors who enforced orthodoxy by exile or execution. The Roman Catholic and Eastern Orthodox authorities resisted modern knowledge and the rise of democracy, in errors not admitted until well into the twentieth century – if then. Protestantism was more favourable to both developments partly because its discipline over its adherents was less effective, but its reliance on the Bible often amounted to fundamentalism in practice, alienating the educated, and the dependence of some of its churches on their national government, or on landlords and employers, often meant an alienation from the millions. A relatively tolerant and comprehensive church such as the Church of England used its influence over a long period to deny civil rights to 'Dissenters', Catholic or Protestant, and did not use it to campaign for the human rights of the poor majority of the population.

In some situations in Europe churchgoing has been quite popular, but after influences more social than religious. The reasons why the poor are alienated may be the very reasons why a church may be viewed with some favour by the more comfortable. A church may be valued as a support for family life and as a provider of education. Or people of different classes and lifestyles may all value it as a symbol of patriotism. Thus Polish Catholicism has been an alternative to oppression by Orthodox or Communist Russia, and British colonial rule has been defied by Irish Catholicism or Cypriot Orthodoxy. The power of Islam has been confronted by Spanish Catholicism and by Orthodoxy in the Balkans. The Orthodox form of Christianity has been preserved in Russia or Greece partly because it has seemed to be bound up with being Russian or Greek – even under the Communists in the one nation and under the Turks in the other. Protestant churches can also benefit by being regarded as carriers of national identity. In Scandinavia the levels of regular churchgoing are very low but the Lutheran churches enjoy high levels of acceptance as parts of national life, particularly in the registration and blessing of births, in the moral education of the young, in the administration of social welfare and in the conduct of funerals. Almost all Swedes, for example, are baptized in infancy and buried by the Church of Sweden.

However, such factors which have operated in favour of church-going may not remain permanently influential. The middle classes can identify themselves without using religion, by the ownership of an expensive house and car for example. As Russian, British or Islamic rule ceases to threaten a population with a different religion, a church can seem redundant in the new nation. In old nations accustomed to freedom the national church can yield to new values and symbols, more international and less ecclesiastical. That seems to have happened to Protestantism in Scandinavia as in Britain, for the popular religious feelings which used to support the national church against foreign Popery can be transferred to Green causes or to football clubs. In Western Europe the total defeat of Nazism and Fascism left the churches in a strong position even where they had not encouraged resistance, and their influence was seen in a new political movement, the Christian Democrats. Yet the churches did not keep their post-war prestige, and leading Christian Democrat politicians eventually drowned in a sea of scandals. In the Soviet Union and its empire over Eastern Europe the churches kept alive a worldview resistant to Marxism, and after Communism's spectacular collapse their contribution was acknowledged. Church leaders might now hope that the religion which had been martyred would triumph but in fact the people have not crowded into the churches. One estimate is that in Russia, after 1,000 years of Orthodoxy, only 3 per cent of the population are regular churchgoers. In Poland, Solidarity, the church-related movement which played the leading role in the drama of Communism's defeat, does not now have a single seat in Parliament.

*   *   *

Most of the rest of the world is more traditionally religious than modern Europe. When the twentieth century began it was quite a common opinion in Europe, and to a lesser extent in the USA, that the century would see the decline of religion around the world, to near extinction. It seemed incredible that progress in its modern form could be either reversed or resisted. Was not science the supreme, even the only, kind of verifiable knowledge, and under its rule was not all religion essentially superstition? Did not psychology teach how desires traditionally respected as religion were in reality satisfied more healthily when there was no belief in an invisible but judgemental God? Could not people be encouraged to be themselves, not obedient to religious laws which were clearly out of date? Did not patriotism for the many, and for the idealists the vision of a world in prosperous peace, offer a better way than religion in unifying and inspiring a nation? But as things turned out, science made possible horrific weapons of destruction, which were used; perceived as unfriendly both to humanity and to the environment, the world created by science set in motion a very large 'back to nature' movement; many of the poor lost hope; many people lost much of the sense that life has a meaning; many found themselves in unprecedented confusion about how to live from day to day, and experiments replacing the traditional family backfired; so in modern societies a God-shaped gap became noticeable. A major development was the emergence of political movements which functioned somewhat like religions: both Nazism and Communism had this character. Less modernized societies could turn to the powerful combination of national pride with a solidly traditional religion, such as the Hindu inheritance. As the century ended, Islam seemed to offer the best hope to the poor from North Africa to Indonesia and the educated were among those returning to their Muslim roots. As the next century began, an anger connected with religion – although the connection was not simple – crashed into New York and Washington.

Christianity was also affected by the religious revival in the twentieth century, but because Christianity had a closer relationship with modernity than most other religions, it faced greater challenges, at least in the short term.

In North America the churches have actually boomed in the modern age and the basic explanation seems to be that Europe's traditions were valued all the more when transported to a continent which could look very frightening – the 'howling wilderness' or the hostile city – yet it was learned that the churches could flourish in the new world only if they operated in a new way. It was necessary to abandon the European pattern in which the state conferred great privileges, and where possible a religious monopoly, on a single church. Instead the churches had to work like everyone else, energetically and competitively, and in religion as in business success rewarded sweat. As the people moved west the preachers moved with them; as new generations of European immigrants flooded into the cities the churches welcomed and sheltered them; as the Black Americans struggled up from slavery the churches supplied friends, dreams, songs and leaders; as the USA was sucked into two world wars, the Cold War and the war against terrorism, the churches were symbols of the way of life which needed affirmation and defence. English or French churches had a roughly similar role in the development of Canada. So modernity proved good for church membership in North America, in a process which is one of the things which Europeans find hard to believe.

The history of Latin America has been very different. There Catholicism in a south European shape was imposed by violence and then maintained by a missionary effort which was too often inspired and staffed from the other side of the Atlantic. It was never fully owned by the people, and when regular churchgoing became voluntary it was not much above the European level in popularity. However, the people usually remained religious in their own way, a mixture of Catholic and older elements expressed in corporate festivals and private practices. Thus it was still possible that the Christian Church would become more deeply rooted in the life of the people, and in the second half of the twentieth century it seemed that this possibility was being seized. In the Catholic Church there was an 'option for the poor' through a theology which proclaimed the people's liberation and through small groups where the poor were encouraged to discuss practical problems with the Bible for inspiration. And the Catholic Church lost its virtual monopoly as the informal enthusiasm of Pentecostal worship provided an alternative to the Mass – and in the signs of being 'filled with the Holy Spirit' as an alternative to ancient fears of other spirits.

However, by the year 2000 it did not look certain that either in North or in Latin America the churches would keep the kind of popularity which sociologists can explain: the story of Europe might be repeated. The reality of daily life in North America has never been one of a simple conformity to the teachings of the churches (as the rest of the world is quick to point out) and the various groups which have used the churches as social and spiritual centres may be finding other things to do on a Sunday morning. Already there has been a decline in support for the historic, 'mainstream' denominations. In Latin America both the Catholic bishops and the Pentecostal pastors have remained, for the most part, authoritarian, and the poor may well feel as they advance that they can do without such outdated leadership – and one problem for the Catholic Church is that the shortage of priests cripples any attempt to teach the people what conservative bishops want priests to teach. This illustrates dramatically a worldwide problem for this very large church: its generals want it to be an army with strict discipline but their strategy discourages the recruitment of officers.

In places where people have so far remained religious in their basic outlook sometimes Christianity has been able to meet their religious needs while also being itself one of the modernizing influences. Indeed, Christianity has recently been so successful in some places that it can seem likely that in its third thousand years its centre will shift to the southern hemisphere, having moved during the second thousand from the Mediterranean to Europe and its North American offshoot. Missionaries went from Europe and North America with religious motives, often sacrificing their lives, or the best years of them, but they took with them modern medicine and education, modern agriculture and technology, and the pregnant idea of human rights despite their own links with political or economic colonialism. They usually found it difficult to make many baptized converts – especially difficult in Islamic Africa and the Middle East, in China and Japan and in Hindu or Buddhist Asia where the existing religious traditions were far more resistant than in southern Africa – but eventually a localized form of Christianity, under local leadership, might provide what was wanted in a religion allied with some modernity. Since Africa and Asia are the continents where most people live, this planting of churches in new soil could offer exciting prospects of growth. By 2000 Africa south of the Sahara had become virtually a Christian continent, with a vitality unmatched elsewhere in the Christian world. In China the expulsion of all foreign missionaries and the persecution of all religions were followed by increased numbers of Christians, and in some non-Communist areas such as Singapore, Hong Kong, South Korea and the islands of the South Pacific the churches were so well established that they could send out missionaries; and with a sense of moral superiority which is now understandable but which would have astonished missionaries from Europe in the nineteenth century, Christian Africa has sent out rebukes to a 'decadent' West. And yet the awkward question must be asked about Christianity's future in Africa and Asia alike, as in the Americas: what will come when modernization has developed further, when modern education spreads and breeds scepticism about all traditions, when modern hospitals are provided by governments, and when watching a screen may seem more attractive than hearing a sermon?

Spreading out from Europe since the seventeenth Christian century, Christianity has become the first truly global religion and modernity has become the first truly global culture. The future will see more interaction between these two forms of globalization and it may be an omen that during the twentieth Christian century the number of Christians in the world trebled – yet did not keep up with the growth in the world's population.

*   *   *

Behind these questions which can to some extent be answered by statistics looms a larger and harder question: are traditional religion and the culture of modernity two worlds, never to be joined?

Traditions can be protected by the whole structure of a society. Especially in a rural community, positions in classes and skills leading to jobs can be inherited; roles in stable families can be performed, perhaps with grumbles but without divorce or rebellion; religious and other rituals can be accepted as what everyone does; and from birth to death life can seem as unalterable as the cycle of the seasons. But the disruption cased by modernity is also obvious.

It begins with the curiosity and scepticism of unconventional individuals but gradually it builds up a whole new house of life. Knowledge acquired bit by bit through the empirical and experimental sciences produces technology which in its turn creates urbanization, mass production, mass consumption and mass culture: first the newspaper, then the radio, then television, then the internet . . . Traditionalists may dislike what they now see but most people do not, for health, education, long life, self-respect and pleasure without censorship can be the experience of the many to an extent previously inconceivable. The modern market exists in order to sell goods which consumers choose to buy, and it does not much matter that many of these goods are affordable because standardized. The modern state exists with the consent of the public in order to fill the gaps left by the free working of the market, and although the bureaucracy is complained about, people do not vote to abolish it, because it suits them far better than any earlier regime. Modernity can be blamed for many problems but massively it is either enjoyed or desired. The history of the twentieth century disproved the myth that progress is inevitable and irreversible – but equally, it contradicted any idea that the 'modern project' has spent its force.

However, the continuing variety in people's reactions to the success of modernity is another obvious fact, because people are obstinately and endlessly different and because in the same person there are conflicting moods. To some people tradition now means very little, if anything at all: to them the old stories are myths, the old customs are habits, the old beliefs are superstitions, the old moralities are denials of life, the old ceremonies are mind-drugging rituals, the old stability is stagnation. But in a modern city a church – or a mosque or a temple – may be a reminder of 'home' and large numbers of people can retain a fairly traditional worldview, indeed a fairly conservative Godview, for use on suitable occasions. What may still be called the soul may not be located within the modern matter-of-fact mentality, and what matters most may be said to be in the heart, which beats now as it always did. TV will go digital but still many of its dramas will be about time-old issues in personal relationships. Young people can combine an enthusiasm for new technology with a reluctance to study the science which made it possible. Older people may be more conscious of the problems which science does not solve than of those which lie within its realm. Such feelings can be released as music if not as arguments. Thus many people want to live in the modern sector of life, in Latin *modo*, 'just now' – but they carry with them from the past something which they did not buy in modernity's supermarket and do not wish to sell.

In the churches, as in non-Christian religions, the reaction to modernity can be a defiant reaffirmation of a familiar tradition – as may be seen to varying extents in Eastern Orthodoxy (heroically immobile under centuries of persecution), in nineteenth-century Roman Catholicism (summoned by Pius IX to an unyielding war against the evils of modern civilization), or in twentieth-century Protestant fundamentalism (battling in defence of the Bible and of a Bible-based life), but still everywhere resistant to plans for change which sound like proposals for surrender to the unbelieving world. The success of Islam in achieving the surrender of many millions to a clear revelation, taught with authority and enforced by law, can arouse some envy.

The case for conservatism in religion deserves to be stated with respect, if only because people's deepest feelings can be involved. It is the case for maintaining a tradition still believed to offer eternal salvation – and also the case for stability and calm in one area of life in a time of many rapid changes and much stress. Integrity is valued but chiefly as the integral preservation of a religious community's traditional beliefs and values because those certainties were what inspired the hope of heaven and, before heaven, a whole way of life which now looks more admirable than modern life – less materialistic, less coarse, less selfish, less stressful and happier, or at least more content. Indignant traditionalists can point to consequences not desired or foreseen when old landmarks were removed: after the modernization ordered by the Second Vatican Council churches emptied; after the criticism of the Bible by liberal scholars the Bible was no longer read; after liberating changes in sexual morality more adults and their children suffer from sexually transmitted diseases, fewer adults know married love enduring until death and fewer children live with two parents. It is not surprising that in reaction it can be felt, powerfully, that modernization should be confined to methods of presenting a message which does not change, that scholars should defer to leaders and should concentrate on making the wisdom of the past available, and that the differences between right and wrong, and between sacred and optional, should be taught more confidently, feeding the sheep and the lambs.

In non-modern sectors of societies around the world traditionalism is reflected in the attitudes of most people to moral questions, and the term 'most people' includes most Christians. In Chapter 5 I shall discuss the traditionalism in the official teaching of the Roman Catholic Church on debates about ethics active in modern times but not at the centre of the Gospel, and I shall agree with the opinions of many modern-minded Catholics who lament that here the teaching is too traditional. Had space permitted, I might have offered a similar critique of traditionalism in Eastern Orthodoxy or Protestantism. And I make no apologies for being on the modern side, which seems to be winning: even in mainly non-modern societies the human rights of the individual are being asserted, women refuse to be treated as servants or slaves, artificial contraception is used when available, and so forth. But those who want changes in the official teaching need to remember that what should be wanted is the honest acknowledgement of the well-informed consciences of Christians with modern minds in modern societies: no less than that, but also no more. It would be wrong, as well as ineffective, to attempt to force changes on traditionalist regions or individuals. It is right as well as realistic when – as is not always the case – modern 'liberals' advocate everyone's liberty.

Within the modern world traditionalism can make a new claim, for it can be called postmodern. 'Postmodernism' can mean many things (or nothing) but when understood as being more than a matter of adding frills and quirks in order to make modernity more entertaining, it is a serious reaction against the modern tendency to impose a monolithic uniformity. It is now seen that modernity must make room for the odd personality and the odd community – and it follows that it must make room for many oddities, since anybody is entitled to say what is 'true for me' as a result of personal experience, and any community is entitled to construct its own world of feelings and beliefs which may or may not correspond with reality as seen in other worlds. It may follow also for postmodern believers that individuals and groups are perfectly entitled to say that what is true for them is 'what the Bible says' or 'what the Church teaches', rather than what scientists (for example) claim in any given period.

It is possible for Christians to think that the Church needs further modernization without rejecting everything believed by traditionalists, and that is my own position. But it is not the position of all Christians with modern or postmodern minds. On the contrary, large numbers of people nowadays develop a defiantly unorthodox spirituality which, as they say, 'works' for them. If they want to be counted as Christians they make a radically new use of the word 'God', stripping away transcendence. What survives from the memory of the God of the churches may be a strong morality. In the eighteenth century the final position of Immanuel Kant, for example, seems to have been that God is 'not a being outside me but a thought within me' – yet he retained the Protestant morality of his main period when he had taught that obedience to the commands of the conscience carried with it beliefs in the freedom of the will and in immortality as a prize bestowed by God. And modern young people who would have shocked Kant by their sexual behaviour can still feel passionately that the pollution of nature is utterly wrong or that cruelty is unforgivable. But this strong morality is not usually connected with what the churches teach about God and may often be linked subconsciously with a pleasure in denouncing sinners who are not oneself.

Nietzsche told the story of the death of God with more feeling than Kant, and looked forward to the coming of Superman to save a Godless world; the Nazis liked the idea. But when the Nazis had gone, a more cheerfully positive and idealistic spirituality welcomed the dawn of the New Age. This age has had as many interpretations as postmodernism, but the central one seems to be that the whole of nature is full of a power which reaches its climax in humanity, with the possible rise of some humans into a still higher consciousness. The connection with Christianity can be that Jesus was the most ascended human yet to be seen but the key ideas are not self-sacrifice but equal self-esteem, self-expression, self-development and self-fulfilment – not Superman but Everybody, standing tall. This 'I'm me' culture is not a plea for ruthless selfishness ('me first'), for there can be a strong emphasis on living harmoniously with other people who are also free to be themselves ('make love not war') and on care for the environment which makes everything possible ('save the planet'). But in the New Age there is no surrender to the God revealed in a tradition, and there is no dependence on the God whose power is conveyed through a religious institution.

*　　　　*　　　　*

These various positions in a chaotic religious situation are, I expect, familiar to anyone likely to read this book, but my purpose in restating them has been to offer some evidence that I have been aware of what is at stake – and that I am not convinced that all truth and all reality lie either in tradition or in modernity. This prologue has seemed necessary because I know that my being in the middle of traffic speeding to the right or to the left can annoy both traditionalists and modernists.

A conservatively Evangelical writer, D. A. Carson, connected me with what he called *The Gagging of God* (1996), concluding that I had no right to claim to be a Christian. A conservatively Roman Catholic writer, William Oddie, also attacked what he saw as my lack of belief in the 'divine inspiration of Scripture'. In *The Roman Option* (1997) he deplored what to him was the fact that I was 'for two decades the most prominent spokesperson and ideologue in England for the sceptical principle within Anglicanism'. He dismissed what I wanted for the Church as an 'ecclesiastical Disneyland' and found it 'quite intolerable' that while destroying so much my tone was 'bland and studiously charitable'.

However, in a book called *Tradition and Truth* (1989) I collected reviews and reflections in which I offered criticisms of some of the modernists of the Christian Left. Attempting (in vain) to start a new fashion in argumentative theology, I included replies by some of those criticized – and found that they could be as angry as Carson or Oddie. I had caused offence by not being sufficiently detached from the Church's tradition. New Testament scholars complained that I had not begun to understand the destructive conclusions of sound scholarship, and an expert on the history of doctrine that I had merely restated an incredible orthodoxy. I was criticized for calling Christianity the best among the world's religions, and Don Cupitt, who thinks God 'non-real', called my values 'demonic'.

Before I try to defend a hope for the future of Christianity which can seem intolerable to some on the Right and demonic to some on the Left, I must offer a defence for being what I am. I am, I suppose, an intellectual and I am aware that few people enter, stay in or leave a religion for reasons which are entirely or mainly intellectual. But if most people support or reject faith because of their own emotional needs or because in their circle that seems the normal thing to do, in the background is the thought that the religion has, or lacks, prestige because of what has been thought true or false by those who have explored, defended or attacked it intellectually. And it is also a fact that rapidly increasing numbers of people think vigorously for themselves about religion as about other subjects – a fact demonstrated by the polls which show doubt or dissent all over the place in the modern world, and also by the many signs of increasing spiritual and intellectual disturbance in traditional societies. So I claim that, especially when religion is in a fluid state, there is room, and even a special role, for an intellectual who is unable to stop asking questions. However, the room is likely to be uncomfortable and the role may be unpopular, for while the traditionalist fellow-members of the religion will protest that the questions being asked about orthodoxy are lacking in respect, critics who are thoroughly sceptical about the religion will complain that the questions being asked about truthfulness are lacking in courage. Being thought too sceptical, or not sceptical enough, has been my experience and although I have had the experience in untypical places I believe that nowadays many who

both 'believe' and question have been through criticisms and self-
criticisms which were not completely different.

*   *   *

As my education progressed I discovered the extent of the gap
between the world of modern thought and the world of the churches'
inherited religion. From an early age it was my ambition to become a
priest of the Church of England – an ambition which troubled few of
my contemporaries – but I held it or, to be more accurate, it held me.
I was born in Cairo, a child of imperialism since my father was an
inspector of schools in Egypt which was then a thinly disguised part
of the British Empire. I must have been influenced when taken to the
little white church in the suburb where we lived but my parents were
not churchy and I was not. My dream at first was to be another
Nelson, for I had been fascinated by Southey's uncomplicated biography of that hero whose victories had resulted in a phenomenon
which I had seen: in Port Said at the end of the Suez Canal I had
watched the liners being fuelled with coal on their journey 'home'
from Australia or India, never stopping in any port not under British
control. But when I went to school in England my eyes were opened
to the Church by a schoolmaster who became a priest in middle life.
I was also influenced by the wartime atmosphere, when the secular-
ization of Britain was halted temporarily and George VI could
summon 'my people' to a National Day of Prayer.

A bit later I was sent to the King's School, Canterbury. It is normally attached to that cathedral, the scene of education for boys
since around the year 600, but during the war it was evacuated to
Cornwall. I was greatly influenced by the headmaster, Canon Shirley.
His rule by the force of personality was no doubt unconventional but
for me it supplemented a curriculum of the Greek and Latin classics
plus English history and it helped me to take to Canterbury's tradition like a lame duck to water. He enjoyed being indiscreet and what
I heard from him about the cathedral's other personalities (for
example, about the dean who was a propagandist for the Soviet
Union), and what I saw in his own complex character, fully persuaded me that not all clergymen are wise men or saints. However, it left
me with the thought that I might be allowed to join them – and with
a boy's enthusiasm for English history as my heritage and for the
Church of England as my extended family. To this day I am thankful
for that – and for the fact that among the books I have written the

one which has been most often reprinted is on Britain's cathedrals which are now visited, used and loved by very large numbers. Only to their full-time staffs do they offer an intimate fellowship, but their doors are open to one and all, and to many, devout or not, their beauty is a sacrament.

Two years of national service in the ranks of the infantry were a further education, this time in realities far from cathedrals, but at Oxford I studied history in Magdalen College and in 1952 won a Prize Fellowship in All Souls College, lasting for seven years. And in Oxford the religion I had absorbed was challenged intellectually.

In Magdalen College C. S. Lewis taught English literature but I was aware that his colleagues disliked his fame as a writer expounding traditional Christianity; they refused to make him a professor although he was eminently qualified. The college's most influential figure was Professor Gilbert Ryle, who made an impact in a limited circle by his book *The Concept of Mind*, destroying the idea that the 'mind' is distinct from the body: it is the activity of the brain, known to others by behaviour. He did not directly discuss religious questions so far as I was aware, but inescapably this kind of philosophy raised problems about the meaning of words such as 'soul' and 'God', words which could seem to be echoes from a distant world of credulity and superstition, a world which the intelligent should forget. I belonged to a troubled young group which began a short-lived magazine as a forum for debate. The first number began with a philosopher's attack on belief in God, arguing that since people cling to that belief despite what they know, it is plainly nonsense and has to die, even if only by the slow 'death by a thousand qualifications'. Believers are like people looking at a rough patch of ground and pretending that it is a garden although the gardener is invisible.

Thus I did not enter All Souls College as a virgin believer. But it was there that the problems of Christian belief in the modern age really struck me. I had time to read and think and I was being examined by a question more difficult than one about the desirability of a lifestyle influenced by Christianity. Should I become a priest, teaching that Christianity is true? I was surrounded by people with some of the best brains in the country and – as was now true of Britain as a whole – not many of them showed much interest in the churches or their doctrines.

The college, which includes no undergraduates, was founded by a medieval archbishop as a place of prayer for 'all souls of the faithful departed' and of training for men who would make themselves useful in Church and State. But it had changed and only one other Prize Fellow became a priest during the twentieth century. I was now tempted in the sense of being tested; every Christian must be, Christ was. I got off lightly, for All Souls College was no wilderness, but in what was a kind of a palace to my eyes, over the wine and under the portraits, the testing came because the men around me, distinguished in public or academic life or rising to distinction, were for the most part politely but obviously puzzled by my wish to be a parson. The scholar whom I admired most, Isaiah Berlin, is recorded in his biography as having said that he had never found any meaning for the word 'God'. *Religion in a Secular Society* by Bryan Wilson, a Fellow of All Souls, was published in 1966 but summed up what challenged me in the 1950s, taking as incontrovertible the conclusions that reasoned theology is now impossible and that religion, whatever may have been its social and emotional roots in history, is marginal in any truly modern society.

There were some undeniably clever people, in Britain as elsewhere, for whom belief in God was not marginal, but if they argued about what 'God' meant to them they could be influenced by an intellectual movement in which the philosopher Ludwig Wittgenstein was the biggest name. In his later years he taught that there are many 'languages' belonging to different 'games' (chosen ways of life and thought which can be intensely serious). In each language there are 'rules' about what is acceptable within that 'game'. Thus a fairly traditional kind of Roman Catholic faith could be defended by Wittgenstein's executor and translator Elizabeth Anscombe, or supporters of Karl Barth's kind of Protestantism expounded in the multi-volumed *Church Dogmatics* could affirm the revelation in the Bible within life in the Church, dismissing not only science but also 'natural' theology outside the Bible and 'human' religion outside the Church. This line of defence for religion anticipated the later development of postmodernism, but I could not be persuaded. Religion-in-general has been better defined by the sociologist Robert Bellah as 'the symbolization of man's relation to the ultimate conditions of his existence'. A particular religion is not a 'game' in any sense, however serious. It may be sung out or danced out rather than thought out and its rituals may be performed without any clear understanding of what they are supposed to signify. Its whole emphasis may be on behaviour, not theology. But it will certainly be regarded by almost all its adherents as a coherent system of feelings and thoughts, and as one which corresponds with, or is compatible with, what may be available of more down-to-earth knowledge of facts. It will be a communal activity but in the background will be the idea that its central beliefs ought to be accepted by everyone because they are true; they are not useful fictions. And in the foreground will be the feeling that what this religion teaches about morality, or at least what are thought to be its essential teachings, ought to be obeyed or at least respected as ideals.

I was more challenged by another movement, which attacked all religion as being obviously untrue. Its clearest exponent was A. J. Ayer, although he later regarded his early, deliberately provocative, work as almost entirely a mistake. In its heyday logical positivism denied that any talk claiming to be about reality must be capable of being shown to be true by the senses and preferably by a scientific experiment (unless it is a statement of logic or a definition of a known entity). All other talk is not only untrue: it is also meaning-less. As this movement grew up it became more aware of the difficulty of proving anything outside the laboratory, and also more aware of the impossibility of fitting into this little box morality regarded as anything more than a preference for certain acts – but it still insisted that a meaningful statement must be capable of being shown to be wrong by experience, somewhat as a scientific theory can be disproved by an experiment. By either test theology was con-demned as 'metaphysics' without meaning, with believers clinging to dogmas which can be neither 'verified' (proved correct) nor falsified. Before developing his 'games' theory, a younger Wittgenstein had acknowledged 'mysticism' as wonder that anything exists, but where logical speech about particular things was impossible he also had urged silence.

I realized that I would not be able to keep silent about God if I was going to become a preacher, but first I had to listen to those intellectu-al giants who between them had created the modern mind. Darwin had shown that *Homo sapiens* had emerged out of a long line of other animals and not directly out of the hands of God; Marx had shown that belief in God had often been used as a drug to keep the brutalized workers quiet; Freud had shown that belief was often an obstacle to rationality and even to mental health – and the Prize Fellow of All Souls elected at the same time as me was going to become a psycho-analyst. And while I began to learn some science, economics and psychology – all subjects for which there had not been room in my earlier education – a friend in the college let me work through his large library of modern poetry and fiction. My mind exploded.

But somehow just enough faith survived the explosion to keep me going forward to ordination as a priest in 1955. It was 'faith' in the sense of trusting, as when a woman trusts her surgeon or a man trusts his wife. In all my agitated reading at this stage the words which impressed me most came at the end of Albert Schweitzer's *Quest of the Historical Jesus*. That book presented Jesus as a man deluded by his expectation of the imminent end of the world until his despair as he died, yet its author was soon to begin his famous life's work as a doctor in tropical Africa. He wrote:

> He comes to us as One unknown, without a name, as of old, by the lakeside, He came to those men who knew Him not. He speaks to us the same word: 'Follow thou me!' and sets us to the tasks which he has to fulfil for our time. He commands. And to those who obey Him, whether they be wise or simple, He will reveal Himself in the toils, the conflicts, the sufferings which they shall pass through in His fellowship, and, as an ineffable mystery, they shall learn in their own experience Who He is.

Nowadays every thinking person who has a person-to-person approach to Christ must, I reckon, be content for some time to be compelled but bewildered – and although one does learn, discipleship always means learning.

*　　　　*　　　　*

In 1966 I had another thought-provoking encounter with secular modernity, although again this was in a setting steeped in Christian history. I was invited to be 'dean' (or senior chaplain) in King's College, Cambridge. So I had to think about the college's relationship with its chapel. The size of a cathedral, this magnificent affirmation of the piety of a king who was almost a monk was the supreme achievement of late-medieval architecture in England, celebrated by Wordsworth as conveying the message 'give all thou canst'. The choir had also been famous for many years and was at the peak of excellence.

During my time there, but in accordance with an earlier plan, the candle-fouled interior of the great church was cleaned and electricity was at last introduced. The sanctuary at the west end was reordered in its paving and furniture, so that a Rubens masterpiece, *The Adoration of the Magi*, could be placed above the altar. I was not such a fool as to think that the traditional worship offered in such a magnificent setting could, or should, be changed more than slightly. I grew to appreciate the classics in English and European sacred music, to love the daily Choral Evensong, and to be excited when the broadcast or televised carol service was enjoyed in many millions of homes around the world every Christmas Eve. How often has the discipline of singing in a choir been a moral, and even religious, experience! How much great or good music has been connected with a religious tradition! How often has music taken people into religion by creating without speech invisible worlds of beauty, struggle, suffering, joy, harmony and symphony! How often has poetry with a religious dimension, spoken or sung, reached people's hearts! And how often has music or poetry become an alternative to a religion now neither loved nor believed! All these thoughts ran through my mind as I stood at the door and people who were leaving paid me a well-intended compliment, although I had made none of the building or the music: 'quite out of this world'.

But I soon learned that the college was separated from its chapel by more than a large lawn. There was a chasm between its music and the students' disco in a cellar, but that was not the most important contrast. Although by tradition the college's deans had been responsible for the students' discipline, it was soon agreed that such supervision had become an inappropriate role for a priest; Christendom was over and the new age which rather rapidly dawned all over the western world in the 1960s brought with it a new morality. This included new attitudes to gender and sex: King's College was one of the first Cambridge men's colleges to welcome women as members (I voted for this change with enthusiasm) and also one of the first to take a relaxed view about sex on the premises between the unmarried (where I saw problems). But there was also a new hope that the practical benefits of modern science could be shared in peace and more widely among the peoples of the world. Students were of course taken through the natural sciences, engineering and economics (Keynes, virtually the architect of the post-war economy, had been a Fellow of King's), but life is not only about facts and in these late 1960s the demonstrations and other disturbances which belonged to the international movement of 'protest' were dramatic.

Elders might laugh as privileged young people with good jobs ahead of them talked of revolution, wearing an icon of a Marxist guerrilla on a T-shirt, and ended up with representation on university committees. But behind these protests by privileged, perhaps naive, idealists could be sensed the very serious anger of the majority of humankind about dehumanizing poverty – and the very serious conviction of many in the affluent North that much remained to be done. I experienced the same mood, differently expressed, when I was sent by the Church of England to the Assembly of the World Council of Churches in Uppsala in 1968: there church leaders were swept into the excitement of a new generation as a new world seemed to be on the horizon. But I knew that to most of the students in my own college, angry or otherwise, the chapel with which I was identified was as remote as the time of its construction.

Adults who sided with the protesting young included the college's head, Sir Edmund Leach, an eminent anthropologist who was President of the British Humanist Association. He refused to read the last lesson in the broadcast carol service, as had been the tradition for the holders of his office, and viewed his college's chapel somewhat as an anthropologist might visit the curious ceremonies of a tribe remote from the modern world. He understood 'humanism' in a sense which made it a systematically Godless religion of humanity, for which he was an evangelist. In 1967 he gave the Reith Lectures for the BBC and these were published under the title *A Runaway World?* He defended the young who 'argue that they are the involuntary heirs of a generation of incompetents' and he received 500 letters in response. These included some applause from Christians, making him anxious to explain that he had not intended to expound 'Christian-sounding moral precepts'. Instead, the beginning of *A Runaway World?* set its tone:

Men have become like gods. Isn't it about time that we understood our divinity? Science offers us total mastery over our environment and over our destiny, yet instead of rejoicing we are deeply afraid . . . All of us need to understand that God, or Nature, or Chance, or Evolution, or whatever you like to call it, cannot be trusted any more. We simply must take charge of our own fate.

Before going to this college I had not paid much attention when warned that a recent dean, a priest who felt isolated, had thrown himself off the chapel's high roof. Now I thought about him quite often. But I must not exaggerate, for angry radicalism was not everywhere at that time and I did not feel completely isolated. In any case, I was sure that the chapel was worth conserving. And I was at least equally worried by the feeling that the theological faculty to which I belonged in the university had made soundings to test the waters in the modern age but had not yet moved decisively to take up the challenge. Leonard Hodgson, who had begun my theological education in Oxford, had once asked a question about the Bible which had become well known: 'What must the truth be now if people who thought as the biblical writers did put it like that?' Cambridge in the late 1960s certainly housed theologians who grappled with that question but their gentle, nuanced learned and hesitant voices did not carry very far into the world of Edmund Leach and the angry, or merely uninterested, young.

So I was glad, although surprised, to get a letter from the Prime Minister in 1970. It offered me another role in a traditional setting, but in a place where I could have more freedom to work at these tough problems of Christian faith and life in the modern world. I was going back to the centre of London where I had already been shown a few answers and where I was going to be shown more.

Ten Books

Recent studies include Grace Davie's *Religion in Britain since 1945* (1994) and *Religion in Modern Europe* (2000) and a more negative verdict was provided by Steve Bruce in *Religion in Modern Britain* (1995). In *Churchgoing and Christian Ethics* (1999), Robin Gill analysed recent surveys of public opinion. In his history of *English Christianity 1920–2000* (2001) Adrian Hastings covered church life ecumenically and magisterially. Recent books which concentrate on the Church of England include Monica Furlong, *C of E: the State We're In* (2000) and Michael Nazir-Ali, *Shapes of the Church to Come* (2001). I offered a 650-page history of *Christianity: The First Two Thousand Years* (1997) and there have been two good recent collections of the views of more detached analysts in the sociological or anthropological mode, *Religion in Modern Times*, edited by Linda Woodhead and Paul Heelas, and the *Guide to the Study of Religion*, edited by Willi Brown and Russell McCutcheon (both 2000).

CHAPTER 2

Glimpsing God

C AN WE EVER GET TO KNOW GOD? Some children seem to find
it easy; some adults think that modernity means *God's Funeral*
(the title of A. N. Wilson's brilliantly clear account of an intellectual
revolution, published appropriately in 1999); and some other adults
assure us that they know him very well and find him very helpful.
But all that I shall claim in this chapter is that the real God can be
glimpsed.

It now seems to me very strange that so soon after taking my
nervous step into the priesthood I was given experiences which
calmed (without completely ending) my inclinations to unbelief.
Mostly I owed my greater assurance to the Student Christian Movement, about which I shall say something in Chapter 6; I served on its
national staff based in London and had discussions all over the
United Kingdom, but my biggest chance to learn came in 1959,
when I was invited to be editor and managing director of the publishing house then owned by the SCM. For 30 years the SCM Press
had already been publishing a wide assortment of theology, popular
or academic, and this continued during my own eight years of
responsibility. Our offices were near the British Museum but we
served people who wanted theology to stay alive.

Our largest excitement came when a young bishop who had been
a biblical scholar in Cambridge wrote a book not to be expected
from such a background: in 1963 we published *Honest to God*.
John Robinson had been shaken by the indifference to the Bible and
the Church experienced in South London, where he was Bishop of
Woolwich, and a period of rest due to back trouble enabled him to
accept our invitation to contribute to a series of paperbacks. He had
become known to the media because he had given evidence in favour
of D. H. Lawrence's *Lady Chatterley's Lover* when a new edition

had been brought out by Penguin, which had been prosecuted for obscenity.

His own paperback touched on sex only when it explained the thinking behind current calls by some theologians for a 'new morality', meaning a new philosophical basis for Christian ethics, but the little book was rapidly denounced as a bishop's further blessing on atheism and immorality. In accordance with the law which decrees that a book which is attacked arouses curiosity, this one sold out more quickly than it could be reprinted. Even those who got hold of it and actually read it could keep the controversy alive because they could quote different passages as saying different things. Readers could contradict each other and it could be argued that the author intriguingly contradicted himself. Soon a million copies were in print around the world.

It was the only occasion in Britain in my lifetime when serious theology has penetrated beyond a small circle. The experience showed that people can still be interested if they come across an honest discussion of the truth about God – and that they do not expect to hear it if they go to church. Many were attracted by John Robinson precisely because he did not claim to know all the answers, and in addition to articulating the questions as they had been forced on him by his own time in secular London he also interested and served the public by introducing them to three greater theologians: Paul Tillich, Rudolf Bultmann and Dietrich Bonhoeffer.

All three were profoundly shaken by the collapse of the civilization to which they had belonged – German, Protestant, cultured and rich. Tillich was an army chaplain in the First World War and was forced into exile by the Nazis in the 1930s; Bultmann tried to counsel former pupils serving in the Second World War and then himself preached amid the ruins; Bonhoeffer was hanged for his part in a plot to assassinate Hitler. Amid the near-suicide of Europe, all three reacted against the dogmatism and escapism of much church life.

Tillich did so mainly in the USA during the churches' wartime and post-war boom. He fell back on faith in God as 'the infinite and inexhaustible depth of all being' – a faith able to overcome the modern condition of anxiety which he experienced acutely. He advised people who thought the word 'God' too debased to be useful to go deeper, asking themselves 'what you take seriously, without any reservation'. That 'ultimate concern' could open up a glimpse of the 'ultimate reality'. If other traditional talk also seemed meaningless, people should ask in each case the existential question, 'what it means for our lives'.

Bultmann's teaching was more focused on the significance of the 'preached Christ'. A leading New Testament scholar, he was passionately concerned to show that the Gospel which had launched Christianity could still reach and liberate people imprisoned in a sense of futility and despair. Like Tillich he has often been accused of leaving God out of the Gospel, but his letter of 1963 to the Sheffield Industrial Mission which I reprinted when I edited *The Honest to God Debate* ought to have ended that misunderstanding. To him the religious question was about Man because it was the question whether Man is truly a creature and meant to live as such. 'The basic sin is . . . Man's intention of trying to live by his own wisdom and power' and the basic human need is to be released 'from all the feverish searching for security and from all resentments and from the complexes which grow out of an unsatisfied need for acceptance'. We can therefore find security and acceptance only if we let it be given by God – and 'the surrender of self-will to God occurs in actual life through loving one's neighbour', before at death we 'hand over everything to God who gives us what is to come'.

Before his execution – 'for me,' he said, 'the beginning of life' – Bonhoeffer wrote letters from prison in which he asked whether 'religion' would have to be forgotten if the Gospel was to reach people with an adult's sense of realism and of responsibility for one's actions in this world. He himself was very devoutly Christ-centred, in prison as previously, but he had been influenced by his experience of the courage of people as heavily involved as he was in the resistance to Hitler while most people in the churches were more conveniently patriotic. In particular he asked whether the picture of the all-powerful God given by so much of 'religion' should be retained at a time of defeat for almost everything that was good. He had come to believe that Christians are called by God to share a little of what God suffers, so that 'when Christ calls a man he bids him come and die'.

When John Robinson presented these three austere theologians to a Britain which had never passed through the darkness that was mid-century Germany, he caused much offence, in particular by the headline which the *Observer* attached to an article in which he introduced his book: 'Our Image of God Must Go'. But what he meant was better summed up by another newspaper's headline, 'God is Not a Daddy in the Sky', or more positively by his own phrases that God is 'the Depth at the centre of life' or 'the Beyond in the midst'. One of those who were initially dismayed was Michael Ramsey, the Archbishop of Canterbury, but his spiritual stature was such that he quickly recovered his balance and saw that Robinson was a Christian wrestling with questions which had become inescapable. In *Image Old and New* he wrote:

> Since the war our Church has been too inclined to be concerned with the organizing of its own life, perhaps assuming too early that the faith may be taken for granted and needs only to be stated and commended. But we state and commend the faith only in so far as we go out and put ourselves with loving sympathy inside the doubts of the doubters, the questions of the questioners, and the loneliness of those who have lost their way.

I have been helped to find answers to my own doubts and questions by many teachers in word or print and I mention a few because, although the work of theologians has so far not reached many of the doubters or questioners, some of it deserves to do so. John Macquarrie has been the best interpreter and corrector of the *Honest to God* theologians and his *Principles of Christian Theology* (new edition 1977) is a modern classic, detaching existentialism from the atheism of Sartre or Camus. Like every other philosophical movement in history, existentialism was influenced by the society around it as well as by the activity in the philosophers' brains. Most of the twentieth century was an agony for most of Europe, when people had to decide either to collaborate with, or to resist, governments or occupying armies which deserved loathing – and had to make, and to go on making, 'existential' decisions which compelled them to work out for themselves what values are supreme in existence as a human being. For Macquarrie the supreme values flow from experience, however fragmentary, of 'Being-itself', by which is meant the 'ultimate reality' about which Tillich taught. And more sympathetically than Tillich, he has shown how every defensible doctrine or practice in Christianity reveals, in its own way, this ultimate reality. There are other revelations – in nature, in human nature, in all the quest for reality in the world's religions – but

Christianity carries the clearest revelation, for here 'Being-itself' is revealed in Christ's human life and in the continuing life of the human Church.

Happily the social conditions which gave rise to existentialism no longer exist in Europe – but decisions about supreme values still have to be made, it is still not completely satisfying to say 'I shop, therefore I am', and the gap in our humanist culture can still be thought to be spiritual and even religious. I therefore mention the teaching of two recent bishops of the Church of England.

Ian Ramsey was a philosopher who went from coping with the intellectual climate of Oxford to be Bishop of Durham and, had he not died at the age of 57 of overwork and heart attacks, he would probably have succeeded the other Ramsey as Archbishop of Canterbury. I wrote a memoir of him because his own life was one of the 'disclosures' to which he appealed in his defence of the use of 'models' in the religious language which arises out of religious experience. He compared religious experience with dedication to scientific work, and religious disclosures with insights after the use of models in science.

John Taylor was a poet who went on from work in Africa which gave him a deep insight into the African religious tradition to be Bishop of Winchester, and to write in retirement *The Christlike God* (1992) with its vision of the God of outpouring, patient, sensitive, active and creative love. He had come to see that only a God of that character could satisfy Africa's religious hunger – only a 'suffering God' in Bonhoeffer's phrase, a God who is not only high but also near, not only active but also patient, not only strong but also sensitive, creative despite many setbacks. That was the God for Africa, a continent with a history of centuries of suffering – the God already glimpsed before the arrival of the Christian missionaries, because Africa has always had what it still has: a sense of the presence of God in all nature and in all human life, living or 'dead'. And Taylor hoped that this would be the God for secularized Europe.

Other theologians have been busy with the positive reconstruction. Archbishop Rowan Williams knows how to relate the past to the present and the future. The faculty of 'divinity' in Cambridge has acquired a new atmosphere as well as a new building and from Oxford have come the books of Keith Ward: even in our age a single theologian can talk sensibly but excitingly about philosophy, science and the world's great faiths. The modern universities of England have produced theology which has been made accessible in the *Oxford Companion to Christian Thought* (2001) edited by Adrian Hastings and others in Leeds. But I must not compile a catalogue of books. Instead, it seems right to concentrate on the key issue, the relationship between modern science and Christian belief in God, although very sadly not only church leaders but also theologians have for the most part not found this problem to be worth their serious attention. Even the theologians recommended in *Honest to God* did not closely relate their Depth or Beyond to science. Fortunately for one such as I am, many good books popularizing science have provided an education in recent years, and the level of the debate about the relevance to religion has been raised in the USA by Ian Barbour and in Britain by Arthur Peacocke and John Polkinghorne; the most recent summary is Peacocke's *Paths from Science towards God* (2001) with a bibliography. Peacocke calls for 'a very radical revision' of what Christians can now hold to be credible and surely he is right in that. Extracts from the literature have been edited by Christopher Southgate, showing by this anthology's title that the scope is daunting: *God, Humanity and Cosmos* (1999).

Since the experts do not always agree, I have had to find my own way through the possibilities – and in this I am like the experts. But the difficulties have to be faced, in reliance on the faith that the Spirit of truthfulness coming from God will set us free from whatever is not true and guide us into all the truth (John 8.22, 16.13). The Church that could be more convincing in modern societies would have to be willing to speak the truth, the whole truth as it sees things, and nothing but the truth as it sees it at present – in these respects, just like science.

*   *   *

The night sky seen by the naked eye is nothing in comparison with what is there. Beyond the 100 billion (thousand million) stars in our own galaxy lies a universe of even more mind-boggling size. It includes curiosities such as superluminous quasars and superdense but invisible black holes, and it seems that a great deal (90 per cent?) of it consists of 'dark' matter which is detectable only by observing its effects on the movements of stars and galaxies. In this universe which is between 10 and 20 (probably about 12) billion years old, light would take about 10 billion years to travel from one end to another – and according to research published in 1998 the universe is still expanding not only continuously but also at an increasing rate, which suggests the very large-scale presence in it of 'dark' energy. If we ask what any Creator may have meant by making all that, the only defensible answer is that we do not know. Nor do we know quite why such a time had to be taken and such risks had to be run if the aim was to produce us. Nor can we tell whether life has evolved anywhere else – and despite exciting suggestions, there appears to be no way of finding out.

If we seek to penetrate what may be called the home life of the Creator, we find that the doors and windows are locked and that despite our hammering there often seems to be no one there. And if that ultimate mystery is inhabited, God must be more real than any thing or any person. As great mystics have said, the Infinite is surrounded by the 'cloud of unknowing', by the 'dark night', by the 'silent desert'. We may feel that we begin to understand God as a power or a person, but that is only because we have to compare the relationship to us mortals with an impact of an object which hits us or with the influence of a person who loves us.

We may begin to understand if God, so to speak, moves on to our ground, and in theology it has been a principle that God is known by his acts, but even then we cannot understand precisely how God 'moves' or 'acts' or 'speaks' or 'reveals' because we have never done what we may believe he has done. At best we can use models and metaphors but soon we come to a halt. We can call God a power or a person, Father or Mother, Creator or Husband, Judge or Lover, King or Friend, Saviour or Sufferer, Mathematician or Artist, Maker or Depth, Reality or Beyond, and we can say that God is above us or upholding us, around us or inside us, behind us or ahead of us, and we can believe that God initiates all events, or controls them, or governs them less directly, or guides them, or influences them, or interferes in them, or lures them on to a good end, or redeems what is not good in them, or lets them be – but we soon find that every metaphor soon misleads and every model soon ceases to cover the ground. We can say that God relates to the creation like a mind controlling a body, or that the creation is God's body, but we find that every way of speaking about our Creator is child's talk. This is not surprising, for we do not know precisely why our own 'self' or consciousness feels distinct from our flesh, or why the human body which is so vulnerable, and weaker than many other animals, includes the brain with the powers of its 100 billion neurons.

Essentially we are a mystery to ourselves, and despite the hopes of some scientists, we seem likely to remain so.

Unsurprisingly, it is impossible to draw on science for an explanation of how the Creator has influenced events in the natural world. It has been suggested that there is a hint of a possible explanation in the fact, now known in quantum physics, that the behaviour of particles smaller than atoms is 'uncertain' in the sense of being unpredictable, because position and momentum cannot be measured at the same time with a high degree of precision: so perhaps God makes things and controls events at this deepest level of all with a skill which no scientist can detect? It is an intriguing idea but one full of difficulties. It suggests that the basic building blocks of the universe continue to be affected instantly by God's direct action, yet normally the processes of creation flow into one another over billions of years. It also suggests that God's opportunity to be creative depends on the existence of sheer disorder, yet order is so normal in the creation that Einstein could make his famous claim that 'God does not play dice'. The elementary particles combine to form atoms with a reliable regularity, and the regularities at the atomic level and above are probabilities so high that for almost all purposes they can safely be treated as laws. Heisenberg, who first reported the sub-atomic uncertainty, and who knew that it is impossible to say exactly when the particles in the nucleus of an atom will disintegrate under pressure, could predict that cities would fall down when he tried to develop an atomic bomb for Hitler.

So can God interfere in things at the atomic level and above? It has been suggested that since 'information' can be fed into a system which is sensitive and dynamic (a familiar example occurs whenever our brains send signals to our muscles by the transmission of electrical forces), God can issue instructions in some such way. But scientists can take this kind of influence into account only if they can detect the initial transference of energy, which is in principle impossible about what is claimed to be a unique act by God. Scientists must agree with the rest of us that the weather is a bit uncertain – but it does not follow that sunshine or rain is obviously the result of an input of 'information' by God to meet human needs in detail. The world's weather cannot be predicted long in advance because the weather systems are influenced by factors which cannot be foreseen with complete precision, but it is not completely chaotic. Events that trigger off results which may be distant have causes which can be

accounted for scientifically, and the weather as presented by the fore-
casters on TV screens is obviously a world away from the world of
pre-scientific faith where it was believed that prayer would procure a
convenient alteration at a particular place and time.

It has also been suggested that activity by God can be spotted in
the results of the interaction between two systems, each of which has
its chain of causes. The most important example is that minor
changes in the otherwise stable structure of genes can produce new
forms of life (mutations) and can result in improved chances of
surviving and breeding when the new form of life enters an environment which has been shaped by a long chain of physical causes. But
the activity of God may still be far from obvious. More often than
not the genetic changes result in the birth of bodies less well
equipped for life – bodies which are in crude terms weak, disabled or
deformed. There can be tragedies which we do not expect to be
caused by a God supposed to be morally superior to us, and there is
certainly waste which we do not expect from a God who is claimed
to be the great Designer. We can reconcile all this with the goodness
of God only if we can put these mutations in a wider context – a
possibility to be explored.

And probably the most familiar suggestion made about the activity of God describes it as the First Cause. It has often been said that
every event must have a cause; therefore, the great event of the
universe must have the greatest of all causes. At first sight this
suggestion is reinforced by the fact now generally accepted by scientists that the universe originated in one 'singularity' – but a difficulty
arises: the singularity was at the quantum level where it seems
impossible to talk of any cause, 'First' or secondary. The unimaginably small, dense and hot 'quantum vacuum' underwent a
'fluctuation' which within a second produced the first particles,
quarks and gluons. Within three minutes the nuclei of hydrogen
could be formed and our universe was beginning to take shape. The
'laws' or regularities of mathematics and physics have operated ever
since that beginning, but about that beginning science can currently
say only that there was a 'quantum fluctuation' with no apparent
causation. In 1965 research was published which reported the detec-
tion of faint echoes of that Big Bang: it was microwave radiation,
spread evenly across the sky, and that was as near to proof as science
can get. But there have been no scientific answers to the question
'who or what caused the Big Bang?' – any more than there have been

religious answers to the child's question 'who or what made God?' All that science can say about the universe is that 'it's there', ultimately an impenetrable mystery not totally unlike the mystery of the God believed to be 'there', with no cause. For science to be able to say more, it would have to able to compare our universe with the 'laws' and histories of other universes – which are not available to be used either in religious arguments or in atheism. The Big Bang may have been the supremely creative act of God from which all existence is derived, but so far as science knows it is also possible that it was just a 'happening'. It was preceded by a 'vacuum' which has been described as energy not containing anything not essential to the existence of that energy. That may be a clue to the truth of creation by the no-thing called God, but it need not be – and in the Jewish, Christian and Islamic traditions what 'creation' means is 'creation out of nothing', so that belief in the Creator would mean the belief that the vacuum was not God but was itself created, God being, so to speak, invisible in the background, somewhat as the author of a drama is not seen on stage or screen.

Whether or not Laplace actually made this reply when Napoleon asked him where God was in all his scientific system explaining the mechanics of the heavens, it is manifestly true that a scientist has 'no need of that hypothesis'. Like a modern historian or sociologist, a scientist when doing a professional duty has an obligation to concentrate on details and to explain them as objectively and as materially as possible, analysing them at a level well below the level where words such as 'God' or 'miracle' or 'mystery' may be appropriate. That will presumably remain the case even if it proves possible to develop a solidly scientific Theory of Everything, as has now become the ambition of some scientists (the most famous in Britain is Stephen Hawking) whose scope is considerably wider than the work usually done in a laboratory. For the scientist, 'Everything' need not include God.

So if He, She or It does not leave any clear fingerprints on the material which is within the realm of science, can God be detected in some other way? Is it reasonable to believe that the Creator is real in any sense at all – although 'real' would have to be an understatement? We can learn from scientists who are also religious thinkers that such a decision is indeed reasonable, although not compulsory. God cannot be seen by looking up a telescope or down a microscope, but I have learned that it is possible to end the sense of the absence of God if we choose to look at the Whole and, with that focus, to glimpse the Depth or the Beyond.

Behind that last sentence are ideas which can be expressed at slightly greater length and hopefully in a clearer connection with science. A physical 'system' can have 'information' fed to it from its own united complexity and not from outside itself, for when its parts combine they may influence each other and then they constitute a new reality. For example, a physical system begins to be alive when chemical processes within it interact and prove capable of producing what is necessary for life. So its own parts make the 'whole', which is a living being. This up-to-date explanation of many phenomena which in the past may have seemed to result from God's interference may now be linked with what Archbishop Frederick Temple suggested back in 1885, that God 'made things make themselves'. It seems that science tells us that, if God is real, this is the main method by which God creates.

When the Creator is called the 'Depth' that image can convey the defensible belief that before anything can exist, and while anything does exist, the possibility of its existence is in the final analysis due initially to the father-like Creator. This Source of all existence may be called the 'Ground' because it is not separate from the creation's existence but is distinguishable from it – so to speak, both inside the creation, present everywhere within it, but also under it, upholding it, somewhat as bathwater may uphold a sponge. This Source may also be called 'Being' because it does not owe its existence to anything except itself; philosophers can call it 'necessary existence'.

It may also be called the 'Beyond' because it cannot be described completely by pointing to any thing, or system of things, in existence; it is, as is taught in Indian religion, *neti neti*, 'not that, not that'. What the Depth, the Source, the Beyond 'lets be' may be glimpsed if we try to see the creation as the Whole, as an unimaginably vast and complex system of interacting parts rising from one level of existence to another – but even then, we point to a mystery, to Being within, beneath and beyond all existence.

*　　　　*　　　　*

Although the brain of *Homo sapiens* has not evolved with the capacity to understand how the Creator works, it is certainly a marvel how much it can understand – particularly through science. In science both knowledge and theorizing are in continual change, yet much stands the test of time. Humans have invented mathematics and algebra and have found that equations have enabled them to carve a way through ignorance about matter which moves at astonishingly high speeds, or antimatter which holds galaxies together, or particles smaller than atoms, or spaces bigger than can be imagined. Using what is familiar, humans have been able to make visual models which represent miniscule realities, as Bohr did with his model of the atom, or invisible models of thought which are the only way in which the universe may be made partly intelligible. And yet what can be discovered reliably through the instruments, equations and models has not made the best scientists arrogant. On the contrary, it has filled them with awe. They have often said that their main motive for their dedication to their absorbing work is their delight in finding ever more examples of nature's grandeur, efficiency and beauty, and if they conceal these emotions behind the claim that they are driven by 'curiosity' that, too, can be an emotion very close to the spirit of religion at its most profound. Their belief that they, their colleagues or their successors will find true answers to their questions implies that regularity in the universe corresponds in some way with rationality as understood by human minds: in the truths about nature are patterns which humans can see, even 'laws' not totally unlike legislation by kings or parliaments. Indeed, the truth-seeking of scientists can put religious leaders to shame. For them, truth is never to be left unexplored because exploration may be uncomfortable or disappointed – and is never to be polluted by any falsification or lazy half-truth. Thus science can have the attitude which in religious language is called worship, and to its work – usually drudgery, sometimes a thrill – can be given a revelation.

But what does the revelation reveal? In his *God and the New Physics* (1983) and *The Mind of God* (1992) Paul Davies conveyed his sense that the revelation of 'laws' throughout nature is an introduction to the Creator who made them – but he has found science more illuminating than any religious doctrine which concentrates on divine interventions in natural processes. At least it can be agreed that the popularity of those books by a professor of physics has shown that there is public interest in the possible relevance of science to the question of God. And the immense interest taken in Stephen Hawking's *Brief History of Time* (1988) owed something to what Carl Segan wrote in his introduction to it: 'This is a book about God . . . or perhaps about the absence of God.'

One relevance of science to religion is fairly easy to state. We have been shown a universe which is from first to last, and from end to end, a unity. Space and time are not ultimately divided: although not quite identical, they are twins in our imagery, and for physics they are a continuum. Energy can be converted into matter and it is matter at work. And there can be no gap between matter and life, for life arises out of an organization of atoms as a delicious smell arises out of a cooked joint. Nor can there be a gap between matter and mind, because the 'mind' is mental activity based on the brain, as music is based on an instrument. This revelation of nature's ultimate unity contradicts old myths which tell how the world was made by different and rival gods – but it neither compels nor contradicts the belief that, as one Whole, the creation comes from the one divine Depth or Beyond.

What flows in all its power and variety from that one source has a structure or is moving towards one. That is why humans can begin to understand what is around them, and even perhaps themselves – and why it does not seem unreasonable to think that the actual or emergent order has a connection with its ultimate origin, since order does not arise automatically out of complete chaos. An optional conclusion is that in the Depth or Beyond of all existence there is reality which to some extent resembles our own reasoning and purposefulness: that is ultimately why what exists has not remained chaotic. So the human exploration of regularities through reason can begin a journey towards knowledge of the 'mind' of our rational and purposeful Creator.

However, the Whole which science reveals does not work like clockwork. Until 1920 every student in Cambridge University had to pass an examination after some study of the semi-scientific theology of an eighteenth-century clergyman, William Paley, unless the student opted to face an examination in logic or in elementary chemistry – and the most memorable image in Paley's teaching was the comparison of the world with a watch lying on the ground in the countryside. Any sensible person discovering it would be sure that a watchmaker had made every part of the mechanism in order to tell the time, and Paley's suggestion was that any sensible student ought to conclude that the world had been made exactly as it is by a divine designer who, in particular, had made human life agreeable. But today it is widely known that the world is what we see because of a very long process of change in which human happiness is not obviously promoted by everything at every stage. Richard Dawkins has therefore mocked the complacent Paley, suggesting that if a divine watchmaker made the world he must have been blind. Yet that quip need not be the final verdict. If we can forget about watches we can now look at the countryside with eyes open to the wonder. Everything we see, in its almost infinite variety and complexity when inspected closely, has behind it a history going back to the origin which is common to all. Everything is changing, perhaps within a day, perhaps within billions of years, but just now everything is here because it occupies a niche, its own place in the sun – and we are here to observe and admire and wonder because very surprisingly we have our own place within what is overwhelmingly marvellous, whether or not we immediately approve of it. That is the world which we humans have to interpret – and scientists have done so, with varying results, when moving outside their professional expertise.

When Charles Darwin was a student in Cambridge, and in the next period before the voyage of the *Beagle*, he accepted Paley's vision of nature without much thought and vaguely considered becoming a clergyman, preaching about God the Designer. His mind changed very famously but in his epoch-making *Origin of Species* (1859) he ended with a vision which still included God:

> Thus from the war of nature, from famine and death, the most exalted object which we are capable of conceiving, namely, the production of the higher animals, directly follows. There is grandeur in this view of life, with its several powers, having been originally breathed by the Creator into a few forms or into one; and that whilst this planet has gone cycling on according to the fixed law of gravity, from so simple a beginning endless forms most beautiful and wonderful have been, and are being, evolved.

Later, that vision faded because Darwin continued to brood on 'the war of nature' with its 'famine and death' in 'the struggle for life', and he felt the difficulty of believing that a human brain, evolved from apes, could find an honest and true answer in which there would be room for the well-meaning Creator. This interpretation of the evidence may well have been influenced by gloomy emotions widespread in the society around him – first, that there would not be enough food for the growing population, and then, that success could not come to everyone in competitive capitalism – but he paid for his epoch-making scientific discovery by many years of a specially acute anxiety about the consequences for morale and morals as the 'descent of Man' from other animals became known to the public. He worried, correctly, that in the next century humans would behave as animals. Yet from that day to this many thinkers who have accepted Darwinian or neo-Darwinian evolution have also accepted his vision of God in 1859, with revisions but essentially unchanged.

Darwin attributed 'variability' in evolving beings to 'use and disuse' of faculties in response to the 'conditions of life', which was why even while his religious vision was clearer than it became it was clouded by the thought of the 'Struggle for Life'. But the modern-minded now have to relate a vision (if any) to the known fact that 'variability' or change in evolution is initiated by genetic mutations which are 'random' in the sense of being unrelated to the given environment, often with bad results. Can there be any grandeur in that view of the physical basis of life? It seems that there can be, for from the play of 'chance' in the mutations the evolution of improved forms of life directly follows. Another result is the evolution of individuals different from their parents – and often different (however slightly) from anyone else in the world. Thus exalted ends can be attained without continuous interference by the Creator. This process was discovered by research on plants in the garden of a monastery in nineteenth-century Austria, but to people who think honestly about religion the relevance probably seems ambiguous. Because improvements often do not result, the verdict can be that life is a lottery without many prizes. Or the conclusion can be drawn that our own emergence as new and individual forms of life is even more wonderful than was thought possible before the science of genetics was born.

The possibility that this more cheerful conclusion is correct has been strengthened by a development in biology since Darwin's day. The emphasis has shifted from his 'Struggle for Life' which awarded prizes to the fittest who survive and prosper because strongest in the struggle for scarce resources. Now biologists point out that new species produced by 'random' mutations can flourish if they behave in a way which need not involve ruthless struggle with rivals. They may be able to cope better with the environment, particularly if it is in rapid and radical change. They may process, store and use information so that they make better use of such resources as are available. They may be more conscious of their own identities, of the dangers which they run, and of their pains which are signals that all is not well. They may co-operate with each other more willingly and efficiently. Their reproductive systems may make them more fertile and they may rear their young with more devotion and intelligence. A realistic view of nature may not see it as a battlefield where victor and vanquished are alike 'red in tooth and claw' as they fight for food: the successful process of survival may be peaceful. Out of this process, not guessed at for almost all of human history and still to some extent surprising or shocking, we have come as a twig on the tree of life.

Certainly this modern, neo-Darwinian, vision recognizes randomness within the regularities – a freedom which seems to run through nature before it reaches us and makes us what we are. And on this view the Creator does not intervene whenever an event occurs which is contrary to the divine purpose. That cannot be expected, whatever we may hope. But even in extreme cases it is possible to maintain the faith that we live and die in a creation where that good purpose can be glimpsed. In 1755 an earthquake devastated Lisbon and wrecked the cosmic optimism of that period. Voltaire used it as his chief exhibit in *Candide*, making a case against the teaching of Leibniz that this is the 'best of all possible worlds', created by the perfect God. But since then science has shown that it is wonderful that Earth's crust emerged out of a very long and very turbulent history – thin and fragile, with moving plates of rock beneath it, yet normally stable enough for a great city to be built and rebuilt.

Even in a still more extreme case, seeing the Whole can mean glimpsing God. When the body-building cells escape from their structures and multiply out of control, perhaps because that tendency is inherited from a parent genetically, perhaps because the victim has lived longer than ancestors did, or perhaps because of a modern habit such as smoking, death by cancer follows unless modern medicine or surgery intervenes. In response, for most of us it is impossible to believe that the good God has decided exactly who is to be the victim – yet not all faith in God need die. It ought not to surprise us that the DNA which is the ultimate physical basis of all living beings sometimes changes: one molecule of it is so intricate that we can be told that it contains more than 10,000 nucleotides. Yet in their many millions cells are normally and wonderfully stable in their structures and when confronting the full dreadfulness of the exceptions to this regularity we may wonder whether a creation without room for cells to be out of control could have ended up in freedom for us. Or if we refuse to consider for a moment such an intellectual response to cancer, we can at least be thankful for the courage, and quite often the faith, of those who suffer. That response in a human life and a human death is a part of the total picture to which we ourselves have to respond: it belongs there alongside the fact of cancer, showing that amid mystery and agony people can be most noble when most tragic. Thus even in the presence of death by cancer, the question of God's reality remains – and with it Einstein's question: 'Could God have made the world any differently?'

Some distinguished recent scientific thinkers – Monod, Weinberg and Dawkins are three well-known names – have concluded that the more the universe is understood, the more it seems ultimately pointless, and it is undeniable that this is a way in which brilliantly intelligent, enviably well-informed and utterly honest scientists can view the mystery of the Whole, inevitably influenced by their own temperaments or societies. But like all the earlier responses just mentioned, it is a response to science: it is not science itself. Science answers the 'how' questions with amazing success, but it ignores the 'why' questions, leaving them to ethics or religion or to unanswerability. Science does not discuss 'the point of it all', positively or negatively. For it, 'value' can apply only to the ability of living beings to survive and breed, and 'purpose' can cover no more than the intentions of living beings. Science speaks about what 'is'. The word 'ought' is introduced into the discussion by ethics, and the word 'God' by religion, although it does not follow that 'what ought to be' has no connection with 'what is' – or that 'God' is not believed by believers to be so real that 'real' is very inadequate. Ethics struggles to answer the question what human life is 'for', a question which to most people is more interesting than any question which science can answer. And religion struggles to say why anything exists rather than nothing. It affirms that existence is not ultimately absurd, and with that answer to nature's ambiguity most people seem to agree, even in secularized modern Europe. They agree – but it is their own decision, neither forbidden nor compelled by science.

*   *   *

Not without difficulty, I am one of those who think that what we have learned about modern science is compatible with the belief that

God, the Source of all that exists or is possible, is the ultimate origin of the immensely long line of events which has produced us. Science does not endorse Hebrew mythology, as some 'creationists' suppose, any more than a fairy story can be shown to be accurate by a report in the newspaper – but much as a newspaper can illustrate truths about human nature which a fictitious story dramatizes, so in its own very different way science can give us truths about nature which can be connected with myths told and retold by people ignorant of science. We know that creation has so far taken considerably more than six days, and so forth – but there is some overlap between science and the myth in Genesis which tells a story about the time between the formless void and the emergence of Man, male and female, from the dust of the earth (*adamah*). I refer to science as now commonly agreed, but of course arguments about God do not depend entirely on this picture being completely accurate.

Nuclear forces neither too weak nor too strong resulted in a history of the universe neither too slow nor too quick from our point of view. About three minutes after the Big Bang the most elementary particles began to be grouped into clusters, made hydrogen and turned into helium: had the nuclear forces been slightly stronger hydrogen would have been rare, and had they been slightly weaker there would have been no helium. After half a million years (or so) the universe was cool enough for atoms to develop, and about a billion years later atoms formed gas and dust which developed fluctuations, at first small, but which by the force of gravity condensed very gradually into galaxies and stars. This process is still continuing but eventually all stars die when the transformation of hydrogen into helium by nuclear fusion is complete. However, when one giant star died heavier elements which had been produced by nuclear action in its interior (including carbon, nitrogen, oxygen and iron) were thrown into space by the mighty explosion and some of them were drawn by gravity to a smaller star, our sun. Eventually they were expelled again by the sun's rotation and they travelled again – this time over a distance where, accompanied by much gas and dust, they began to build our planet. The distance made possible the very slow and gradual emergence of life, dependent on the sun's energy during a very long time when the sun's output was relatively stable. The size of the planet, affecting the speed of its rotation, and the pattern of its orbit around the sun, producing the seasons of the year, were also right. And this planet produced a magnetic field which was a shield from life-destroying rays from the sun.

In Earth's history of at least four billion years, conditions were hostile to the emergence of life for many hundreds of thousands of years. Although the bigger planets attract most of the comets and asteroids, this one was bombarded by many objects from space and the development of its own material was also violent and prolonged. Eventually about three quarters of the surface were occupied by water and the disintegration of the rocks in the remaining quarter produced sand, and after enrichment by organic matter, soil. The plants now able to grow produced oxygen which eventually made up a quarter of Earth's unique atmosphere. The very long story of the birth of life is known in part: the elements of Earth's surface and its early methane-rich atmosphere combined to yield amino acids, which in their turn built up complex replicating molecules, leading to the proteins and the nucleic acids which control the proteins. Filaments of DNA-like molecules functioned independently and living beings were born – although such beings could not be born in Earth's present atmosphere. Some beings proved capable of moving in water. Fish developed backbones, jaws and fins, and their remote descendants flew and walked on land, with mammals emerging about 180 million years ago. The reproduction of life became more complex when done by sex and made possible differences between individuals. At least three million years ago hominids stood upright, used some tools and made fires. As their brains grew, hominids evolved into *Homo sapiens*, perhaps some 400,000 years ago, although humans who can be called 'modern' in some sense, with developed mental powers and cultural activities, seem to have emerged only some 60,000 years ago.

This planet is not always bright and beautiful, but when we look at photographs of our home from the moon it can be seen that what is most marvellous is not the presence of men on the moon but the presence of *Homo sapiens* on Earth. If anything can make us wonder, this can – whether or not the whole astonishing process is brought home to us by the birth of a baby.

It is a pity that in the worship and teaching of the churches the wonder of the creation is not proclaimed more prominently than it usually is at present – and proclaimed with an unsentimental awe in the presence of mystery and majesty. Some hymns have begun to meet the need but in the spoken words there is still too much talk about the 'God who made the world' like a garden instead of the

God who makes the universe – and too little talk about the Creator in comparison with the Saviour (who talked about the Father rather than about himself). Too often is the divine Spirit domesticated within the churches, instead of being the power with which the Creator breathes life into all that lives. And the art in churches almost never depicts and celebrates the energy of God in evolution. The churches miss opportunities to put more reverence-and-joy into their worship, and although they do something, they could do more to appeal to a feeling which now spreads more widely year by year, particularly in the younger generation – the feeling that our planet, made so marvellously over such a long time, needs to be rescued from our greed. Here, in our time, is an elemental and extremely powerful instinct, the very stuff of which religion is made. Christmas and Easter celebrate Christ, and Pentecost or Whitsun celebrates the Holy Spirit – but why does no festival with the same status celebrate the Creator, developing the harvest festivals which have had a deep significance in rural societies but now, in country and town alike, proclaiming the wonder of the creation revealed by modern science?

*   *   *

It seems clear that Christianity is only at the beginning of the exploration of the relevance of modern science to some age-old questions about belief in God. I am going to outline some suggestions which will sound crudely dogmatic but only, I hope, because of the need to be very brief since I am aware that my thoughts are not original or well expressed or well developed.

I begin by confessing that I am one of those who are suspicious of attempts to relate God directly to particular events. In the 'creationist' movement (or refusal to move) in the USA some knowledge of science can be combined with a mastery of modern media in order to dazzle the viewer (if not the thinker) with great marvels which, it is claimed, prove that the Creator is a miracle-worker. In many earlier ages stories were told of smaller (perhaps trivial) events in public history or private lives which, it was confidently claimed, were miracles – and such claims are still made when recommending 'faith' to those who have not had such happy experiences. But the celebration of God which I find most impressive comes when the Scriptures of the world stress the mystery: the Eternal is in eternity, we are on Earth, we should be grateful for what comes to us mysteriously without being absolutely sure about how it arrived. And the attitude to God which I find most admirable is one of humble awe and of a trusting (not knowing) adoration.

It seems to follow that if our prayers are to make sense they should not be non-negotiable statements of our wishes, like a list made before shopping. It is better to devote most of the time to contemplation of the majestic mystery of God and to absorbing the wonder of knowing anything at all about him – and the Lord's Prayer shows that this hallowing of the Name can be a worthwhile exercise even if it is brief. Reminding ourselves that we are in the presence of God calms us and produces in us some awareness that we are small and silly, and also very fortunate. Then it becomes appropriate to remember what we and others need, entrusting ourselves and them to this parentlike Creator whose purposes are both supreme and good. According to the teachers who know best, such prayer does not need many words, since God already knows what is needed, but petition makes us feel our dependence and intercession voices our own loving concern and increases it: whether or not prayer changes events, surely it changes us. In many of our moods prayer is difficult, but gradually we want to pray if we believe, and slowly it becomes as natural as breathing. One thing is therefore necessary in the Church we hope for: it must be a school teaching sensible prayer.

It can be suggested that we should cut through the mysteries by a decision that there cannot be any special acts by God. In the seventeenth and eighteenth centuries this position was called Deism and its clearest exponent was a Jewish philosopher, Baruch Spinoza. Professor Maurice Wiles has presented it more recently (although not exactly in Spinoza's form, since he is a Christian) and when I questioned him in my *Tradition and Truth* he responded by affirming that

> God is active against evil in the only way in which it makes sense to speak of special divine activity within our world – by the inspiration of men and women to work for the overcoming of evil and the creation of that good which is the goal of the whole creative process.

In his *Reason to Believe* (1999) he expressed again the conviction that 'God is not a magician who adjusts the particularities of life at our request, but God is one whose loving presence has the power to transform our experience of every eventuality of life.'

But that is too simple, I believe. That God is active in this way I do not deny: I think I have experienced it. But there are reasons to doubt that this influence over emotional reactions and human work is the only influence which the Creator allows himself. Our brains are physical no less than our arms and legs; without them we cannot either experience or work; and if God cannot be active in influencing matter, then he cannot be active in influencing us. (I shall use 'he' about God without the quotation marks which would be an explicit reminder that God is not a man – but only because of convenience.) And if the Creator had to wait until *Homo sapiens* had evolved before he could influence events after the Big Bang, then he had to wait for more than 10 billion years in the hope that things would work out. It seems more reasonable to believe that if the Creator really began what exists the activity has never ceased to be creative within it. This is different from believing in a God who from outside often intervenes, brushing aside the regularities in nature or history in order to meet emergencies. The real possibility seems to be that God acts either always or almost always not against but through these regularities, exercising his influence not by a 'quick fix' but through the steady pressure of a complex system, a 'whole', on its constituent parts.

In fact modern science was born out of the conviction that God's creative activity deserves study by humans with all the care possible, although much in it will remain mysterious unless humans are given a revelation outside science. Although other factors contributed, the emergence of modern science in a Europe where the culture had been saturated by Christianity was no mere fluke. In the vitally important early years most of the scientists were also deliberate and devout Christian believers: Copernicus was, Galileo was, Newton was, and the list could be impressively expanded. Science was valued as the honest, close and successful study of the Creator's work outside what was recorded in the Bible or experienced emotionally. The world was itself a revelation of God through the 'Book of Creation'. It was to be revered but not feared, and it was to be used according to the Creator's good purposes. But obviously the link between religion and science should not remain as it was in the days of the great founders. Copernicus could only advance a theory; Galileo's telescope could make visible only a little; there were gaps in Newton's science which had to be filled by his belief in the God of the gaps. So what can we now say religiously about what scientists can help (not force) us to see?

In the absence of knowledge we can think it logical to say that the creation minus the Creator would be nothing but that the Creator minus the creation would be divinely blissful. Yet that may not be all that can be said. Creativity on this utterly astounding scale calls for some exploration and it also seems logical to guess that in some sense the creation is necessary to the Creator, for a divine nature which includes creativity needs fulfilment through creation. If all that exists or is possible makes no difference to God, it is hard to see why we should care whether or not God is real. But clearly the form of this creation is contingent, not necessary: things might have been different and scientists can have fun in working out possibilities.

The form taken by creation in this universe and this planet can be understood to a very remarkable extent. It can persuade many humans that the process was intended to include *Homo sapiens*. But other humans are able and entitled to think that we just happen to be here – and of course the central reason why existence can be thought to be, in the last analysis, no more than a large series of happenings is that many phenomena in nature, and many experiences in life, do not look like the work of a God who combines 'almighty power' with equally measureless love. So what can be said reasonably by believers in a God who is not impotent – yet also not beyond criticism?

At least the problem of evil, which must trouble anyone capable of adult thought, helps us to define what ought to be meant by 'God'. The word should not be used as another word for 'nature' if we take seriously our own moral sensitivity, for there are many terrible reasons why it can be thought that nature is ruthlessly pitiless. 'God' should be reserved for the possibility that there is One 'beyond' and 'above' nature as well as 'within' it, the One thought of as 'holy, holy, holy'. The problem is, of course, how to relate that One to the evil or disorder in nature, and it seems that the answer must include the point that the 'omnipotence' of God cannot mean that God can do anything, for he cannot go against his own nature or against what may be called his policy for his creation.

Very many things suggest that this policy is neither dictatorial nor totally risk-free – and that since it has been God's policy to give the creation novelty through freedom, that has produced a package to which we owe our own freedom and, indeed, our own existence through evolution. To prevent the utterly evil Holocaust would have meant God being a dictator himself, exercising detailed control over

European history, where antisemitism sank lower and lower to this ultimate iniquity. To prevent a child's tragic death would have meant that our non-dictatorial God could not have made the world into which the child was born. Once embarked on the kind of creativity of which we have evidence, the Creator must stay within the limits of what he has made possible. It does not follow, however, that we can be certain what the limits are. Some events called 'miracles' in the religious sense may be possible even when most stories about such events are legends. It is obviously foolish to rely on them instead of on processes within the natural order, but it seems not appropriate to rule them out altogether; we may not wish to take that impertinent step if we stand in awe of what God has done by his normal methods.

I have accepted the argument that, despite everything which we think is evil or disordered, the picture of the creation taken as a whole suggests that it is being created for a benevolent purpose which involves humans. I now want to accept another argument: that seeing how much risk is involved in the creativity of this God can suggest that his greatest purpose is to win the love of humans who are left free not to love. They are free not to love God before they die. They can reject the kind of life in his creation which he wants for them, because he wants persons whose personalities have been shaped by a long series of free choices: he does not want robots. And they are free not to love God when they have died. They can reject the eternity which he now offers to them, because he wants personalities who can enter his own life which has love at its heart, love being the free choice of another: he does not want conscripts.

It seems to be no accident that the history of evolution so often leaves the impression that the Creator is, so to speak, experimenting. It has been claimed that God's 'omniscience' must mean that he knows the future, but that is logically impossible, for the future is not 'there' to be foreseen: no one, not even the all-knowing God, can know more than there is to be known at present. It is logically possible that he knows all the present possibilities and probablilities but he cannot know their final outcome for certain. This means that the ultimate triumph of God, often said to be certain, cannot be known in advance. What can be known, or glimpsed, is that God has decided to limit not his goodness but the exercise of his power. Because God is infinitely good it seems reasonable to hope that in the end his goodness will attract everyone willing to be attracted, but because he does not wield unlimited power it also seems reasonable to believe that to the end people will be left free not to be attracted. However, the decision will be theirs, not his: his judgement will confirm their own. We have no need to agree with the ghastly idea that God predestines some, many or most to what is called hell.

It has also been claimed that God's 'eternity' means that he cannot change; so to speak, he is a very impressive statue. But in that eternity there must be something somewhat like the time which we know, for otherwise God's thoughts and actions could not be placed in order. And God cannot be the Unmoved Mover imagined by philosophers such as Aristotle, for science has taught us that his active creativity must be continuous if it is real, and history has taught us that the Creator, if he exists and if we can call him good, must be active in response to the free actions which he has allowed in his creation. If our actions do not matter to him, there would have been no point in the gift of freedom. Indeed, his sensitivity must be greater than ours – in the enjoyment of what is good, in suffering because of what is not good, in the assurance that the outcome will be as good as is possible in a creation which to the end allows freedom.

What cannot change if it is ever true about him is God's goodness, and our deepest human relationships teach us that love which is good and creative cannot command. In a good friendship or marriage there is no boss. In a good family, parents have to learn to 'let be' and in the end to 'let go' for the sake of the love which includes freedom. And other human experiences are also instructive. The director of a film cannot be a dictator over the personalities of the actors and the writer of a script is not in complete command over the behaviour of the characters if the plot is to be believable. I have learned from being a writer of non-fiction (I trust) that the work begins with a plan but the plan is always altered. Possibilities have to be explored; experiments have to be cancelled; other developments are seen to be possible; slowly, one reaches the conclusion after much rewriting. And one does it because one loves it. I have also had the experience of being a manager (on a small scale). One has an aim to achieve a task; then one has to learn what are practical possibilities, given the human nature of oneself and one's collaborators and the limits of the other resources; a strategy must become tactics if the end is to be anything like a victory. And the reward comes during the process, not only in the sense of achievement. I imagine that much the same experience of being a creator but not a dictator is shared by the musician who improvises, by the artist who moves a vision onto a canvas, and by the designer who has to embody an idea in materials. No human creator pushes a button and sits back to await results. This proves nothing about God but it is what we know when we say 'create'.

I shall now get more personal (although not anecdotal) as I return to a point already made theoretically.

I have also had the experience of tasting tragedy, and of knowing that very many less fortunate people have had a full meal of it – an experience which leaves one both unable to speak sensibly and wanting to say something. A tragedy is not what follows our mistakes proportionately: it is what overwhelms us when the degree of evil is not thoroughly deserved punishment. Amid such experiences we can complain to the God who is both powerful and good – and if we do not believe that such a God exists, to whom can we complain? And presumably such a God does not complain about our reaction which is neither unnatural nor unreasonable. But when our protests grow less bitter they may grow less angry. We may begin to know at a deeper level that to be a living being in a species more complex and 'advanced' than others entails being more sensitive to physical and mental pain. We may begin to see that our experience of things and people being free to harm us belongs to the process which has produced our own existence, sensitivity and freedom – and that our experience of having to confront evil with courage belongs to the process which has developed us morally and spiritually up to this point. Our pain may be what is needed to make us more sensitive to what others suffer; indeed, it may actually enable us to help others who have to walk in the dark. And we may be given in our darkness a clearer light, seeing now that as a whole what we have experienced is good. We may speculate that a less hurtful world would have been better for us, but we cannot know that it would have been possible – whereas we can know that what has been possible has been something for which, on the whole, we can be grateful. We can take it, or leave it by suicide, and usually we choose to take it. Thus we can believe, even in the darkness which remains, that the creation is ultimately not evil or absurd; that it is on the whole a good creation because we have a good Creator; and that Augustine was right to teach that 'God judged it better to bring good out of evil, than to allow no evil to exist'. That is not an intellectual solution to the problem of evil but it can keep one going.

*   *   *

To what end do we go? We know that all living individuals must die and that our form of life cannot last for ever because it depends on the sun. One day, now billions of years in the future, the sun's own death will begin. First it will cool, making this planet uninhabitable; then its gravitational activity as a 'red giant' will suck this planet back into itself; then all its activity will end, reducing it to a size like a planet's, as a 'white dwarf'. Depending on what will be its size in the immensely distant future, the universe may expand for ever but as the force of gravity diminishes nuclear fusion will diminish, with an ever-diminishing power to make the scattered stars active – or gravity may pull everything together into a second and final 'singularity', the Big Crunch. That fireball might in due course expand again, with or without different regularities, but of that we know nothing. Nor do we know anything about 'minds', 'bodies' and 'spaces' different from the ones we do know, so that all speculations are non-sensical. There have been other highly imaginative hopes that with the bodies which they already possess humans will contrive to postpone their extinction by travelling to another planet able to sustain life, but that too is the stuff of science fiction, not science.

In a report in 1995 the Doctrine Commission of the Church of England urged that scientific predictions of eventual collapse or decay for the whole universe 'are to be taken with the utmost seriousness' – and then taught that 'Christian hope must be cosmic' since 'matter matters to God and it will not be abandoned to futility'. Although it granted that 'the language in which Christian hope has been expressed is necessarily imaginative and pictorial', the commission thought that such language refers to 'the eschatological transformation of the old creation' into 'a universe animated by God's Spirit, in the most intimate connection with its creator'. But what on earth this means I do not know, since I live in a body and on a planet both of which will die, although this body, this planet and this universe are, I believe, already 'animated by God's Spirit' in an existence which is physical and therefore, for every entity in it, mortal.

However, there is permanent truth in Paul's vision: 'the whole created universe is waiting with eager expectation', even 'in the pangs of childbirth', until its story is fulfilled in the 'glorious liberty of the children of God' after 'liberation from mortality' (Romans 8.19–23). He may have imagined Earth and the stars being glorified in that liberation of humans, but fortunately he did not attempt to make an exact prediction. While science is compatible with Macbeth's belief that the whole story ultimately signifies nothing, it is also compatible with the belief that while all that is material dies, what is valuable in the story, including what is good in us, will be treasured for ever by the Creator where existence began, which is outside space/time and energy/matter. And we can already begin to experience eternity in rare glimpses when the ego of selfishness and wounded vanity is forgotten but the self, however small, feels accepted and fulfilled in moments when we stand very humbly before natural grandeur and beauty, or before human love in its glory, or before great music or art, and the experience is so intense that 'time stands still' because many moments of time are concentrated into this one 'eternal' moment. These moments are usually as unexpected as they are unexplained; they are given, not earned; they are remembered as the most revealing minutes in a lifetime; and like the sense of our physical dependence on the material universe, they are stuff of which religion is made. They can be interpreted as glimpses of what matters most to us – the mystery that there is eternity beyond time, that mortals matter to the eternal God, that as is said in the gospels, the Creator 'is' the God of Abraham, Isaac and Jacob since 'for him all are alive' (Luke 20.38).

In *After Death?* (1999) I tried to sum up a lot of listening, reading and thinking – not only as an old man, but also in a lifetime. I wrote about the human need to come to terms with mortality – a need demonstrated during my work on that book by a nation's open mourning after the tragedy of Princess Diana. I studied the changing face of death and the changing pattern of grief with the help of anthropologists, sociologists, philosophers and poets. When I emerged from that rich world of myth, thought and symbolic action I found it impossible to take literally what has been taught and believed about the soul as a little person easily detachable from the body, or about the body as flesh which will be raised into heavenly splendour, or about hell as endless tortures for the majority of humankind, or about heaven pictured as an emperor's court with years in purgatory as the entrance to the palace – a painful time compulsory for all except the few. But I ended with the affirmation of a faith which seems sufficient for the necessities of living or dying.

It is not a 'faith' in the sense of accepting certain rules or propositions taught by a religious authority, although 'faith' has often enough been understood in that sense in the history of the religions, including Christianity. It seems to me impossible to believe in a God who would leave the evidence for his reality, purpose and power seeming so unclear to so many people – and who would yet be entitled to demand assent to clearly defined rules and propositions as the ticket of entry into heaven. The only kind of faith which seems necessary before the final vision of God is a quality of personality which presumably can be awakened by death as well as by life – a quality of longing but also of ultimate trust found in those who know their need and sorrow, their hunger and thirst, with hearts which are pure, or can be made pure, in the search for a blessing (Matthew 5.3–8).

What is given to people like that can be called 'heaven without another world' – because it must be no-thing, so that all images or words about this ultimate reality must fail as descriptions. But there can be God, the God who loves the persons who are the climax of the creation of this planet because, unlike other animals, they are free to accept or reject a personal relationship with their Creator. A human parent's delight at a baby's response to love may offer a very small analogy. And the God who loves persons can love them to, and beyond, death, somewhat as a human parent 'never gives up'. And what is treasured beyond death is nothing less – but also nothing more – than the personality. Here again the human experience of loving parenthood may offer a faint clue: a child's performance matters at the time but depends on many things which the child cannot control, so that what is valued and remembered most is the character shown in the response to the challenge. But it seems to be more fearfully true that the Creator's gift of freedom can extend ultimately to the acceptance of a free person's refusal to return love, somewhat as a human parent can accept a rebellious adolescent's right to make a very serious mistake or even to break off the relationship entirely. And this possibility can be believed in along with the hope that it will never be more than a possibility, since in the end every person, one by one, will exchange self-centredness for a total dependence on the Reality from which all existence has always been derived.

*　　　　*　　　　*

That hope goes far beyond what is taught by science and all that can be reasonably claimed for it in connection with science is that the Creator's willingness to love and uphold personalities in eternity is not incompatible with any of the material covered by science. But the story which science tells us is the story of marvellous complexity made possible by the production of novelty through factors including some randomness within the constraints of general regularity, and the story leaves us with our own brains as the most complex structures known. And at this point religion can begin its own story, with its claim that although the Creator's dealings with the material creation, and with non-human life, and with us, are for the most part hidden, human brains are such that to them can be given revelations which are supremely worth having. These revelations about what the Whole 'means' have come in moments within very many ordinary lives, and more substantially and over longer periods in the lives of saints and sages around the world. And it is claimed that a human being who is very exceptionally, even uniquely, open and obedient to signals and energies from the Depth or the Beyond is able to share what is given. Above all, it is claimed that such a human being is able to show, by sharing human and other suffering, that there is suffering also in the Depth or the Beyond – but suffering which in the end, beyond all the tragedies, is not defeat.

The Church that could be in contact with the minds and hearts of modern societies would therefore have to speak about the mysterious universe – about what cannot be understood and about what can be, about the unity, the regularity and the freedom seen everywhere, about the wonder that humans have been evolved on this planet, and about the Creator partially revealed in the creation. The Church would have to celebrate this creation by well-informed teaching, by imaginative acts of worship, by sensible prayer in private, and by a passionate love and care for what has been created, since the Church would believe not that God controls everything but that God creates, loves and cares with a passion greater than what is possible for us to be or to know. But of course the Church would also have to proclaim with conviction the truth about Jesus, a man not totally in control but also not defeated, a passionate man whose strange victory reveals the ultimate reality.

CHAPTER 3

Meeting Jesus

A LWAYS AND EVERYWHERE, despite the great diversity in doctrines, practices and morals, Christianity is a reply to one question: 'And you, who do you say I am?' (Matthew 16.15). A lot can be learned from reading and thinking but I am typical in that I have learned most by meeting what Paul called Christ's continuing 'body' – the Christians. Near the end of the fourth gospel Thomas, previously a sceptic, is invited by Jesus: 'Reach your finger here, look at my hands. Reach your hand here and put it into my side.' I do not know that this conversation took place in history: it comes in a gospel which is not usually matter-of-fact. Nor do I claim that all Christians have always left a good impression on everyone else. What I do know is that I have in a real sense met Christ by watching the hands of Christians as they have carried on his work and sometimes by being allowed to go quite deeply into their pains.

If I were to name all the people who have shown me Christianity in action this would have to be a much longer book, but a decisive experience for me was being a part-time curate under a vicar who radiated and received love, Austen Williams at St Martin-in-the-Fields. The church began as a chapel for the countryside between London and Westminster in the Middle Ages. Rebuilt with eighteenth-century elegance by James Gibbs, it became the parish church of a crowded slum but also had a fashionable congregation. Then a gently charismatic vicar, Dick Sheppard, opened the extensive crypt with its many basement rooms to the soldiers waiting to go to the trenches in the First World War, and more recently the church has maintained a large 'social service' unit. It was the first church in England to broadcast regularly and that helped to attract and encourage many who, while not destitute, were lonely and uncertain. When London became international it did too. It also gathered a community of regular supporters who built up a family life while down the steps leading up to the church millions came and went in Trafalgar Square.

I met Christ in this parish church's response to human need in the centre of London. However, I have had to face the question whether in reality I had met not the Christ who 'was' some 2,000 years ago and who 'is' today – but merely the image of Christ the Social Worker, an image which says more about ourselves than about him.

The variety in images of Christ is a familiar fact which can be said by harsh critics to show that Christianity is entirely the creation of people's imaginations. The image which nowadays means most is probably Jesus the Friend and Helper but this can easily be debased into Jesus the Assistant who encourages us to be happy and to do what we want to do anyway, or Jesus the Best Buy who is eager to make us as healthy and wealthy as is the preacher who recommends the product. More political are the Jesus of the Right who teaches that what people need is moral discipline when not making money, and the Jesus of the Left who is progressive but not very religious. A less troubled age favoured Jesus the Philosopher full of common-sense, who told charming stories in order to recommend a supportive belief in a benevolent Creator and a morality which was surprisingly enlightened. Other images were more formidable: Jesus the Apollo-like Shepherd alive among the graves in the catacombs, Jesus the tough young Anglo-Saxon warrior in *The Dream of the Rood*, Jesus the Byzantine world-ruler, Jesus the medieval king who is nevertheless persuadable by his nicer mother, Jesus the most beautiful baby and man in the whole of the Italian Renaissance, Jesus who suffered under the wrath of the Father as Luther suffered, Jesus the Saviour of the predestined few including Calvin, Jesus the censorious Puritan, Jesus the midwife of the convert's painful second birth, Jesus the emperor reigning from Europe, Jesus the anti-capitalist agitator, Jesus the ecofeminist protesting against men's mistreatment of women and of Mother Earth . . . but if I was to believe that Jesus reveals the Truth, I wanted to get at the truth about him.

Other religions have much spiritual power and wisdom to offer but Christianity stands or falls with the one called Christ, the 'power of God' which seems weakness and the 'wisdom of God' which seems folly (1 Corinthians 1.24, 25). Other organizations can provide many of the services which the churches offer, but only the churches exist because of the story of Jesus. That is why it is deeply disturbing that in a time when there is great interest in Jesus, what people hear about him from the churches, or think they hear, is so often found unconvincing. Instead there is a public for theories about Jesus which defy not only the teachings of the churches but also the conclusions of careful scholars. The appeal of these theories is that they appear to be more honest than the dogmas of the churches, and I am unable to refute the widespread idea that many sermons do ignore modern scholarship in the belief that this is controversial and out of place in a pulpit. Nor can I deny that the use of the Bible in the officially authorized forms of worship usually seems to be untroubled. But surely it is possible to venerate Jesus – and to preach about him in a way which is appropriate in the context of worship – while being also faithful to the facts as most modern scholars would accept them as being either certain or probable. The best brief account known to me is *The Historical Figure of Jesus* by E. P. Sanders (1993). Now I want to offer what I think are the facts which ought to be acknowledged and which ought to be enough to inspire a distinctively Christian faith which is compatible with everything that is known.

If we were not so used to this fact, it would astonish us that no one in the history of the world can be named as having been more influential than this carpenter who was executed after a controversial public life which according to three of the gospels included only one of the annual Passover festivals. He wrote nothing known to us apart from some unrecorded words in the sand according to some copies of the fourth gospel. He taught by short stories and sharp sayings and his style was vivid, exaggerated and witty, rather than precise; he was a visionary. He made no detailed plans for the future but instead hoped for the quick completion of the 'kingdom of God' – and he did not define what that would mean. His personality was a combination of what are usually thought to be opposites, so that the evidence resembles a jigsaw puzzle and the variety in later images of him is understandable. He was morally very demanding, yet friendly with 'sinners' such as prostitutes. He was also friendly with the tax-collectors who served a colonial regime and who kept many of the takings, yet he identified himself with the oppressed peasants and led a movement which was in its own way revolutionary. He urged moneylenders to forgive debtors but compared his heavenly father with a landlord. He could be called a glutton and a drunkard, yet he expected great suffering for himself and his followers. He was a devout Jew, yet he denounced the religious leadership of his own people. He was a teacher of 'wisdom' whose whole emphasis was on forgiveness and love inspired by faith, yet he was condemned to the most degrading death imaginable as an actual or potential rebel. He cannot be fitted into any category and of him it has been said that he could not be pinned down in a tomb.

*   *   *

The secret of his influence is contained in the traditional acclamation 'Christ is risen!' This is what Paul said had been the experience of his conversion, it seems about five years after the crucifixion: 'God chose to reveal his Son in me' (Galatians 1.16 in the closest translation of the Greek *en emoi*). It led him to enter what he called 'life in Christ'. He added: 'I have been crucified with Christ: the life which I now live is not my life, but the life which Christ lives in me; and my present mortal life is lived by faith in the Son of God, who loved me and gave himself up for me' (2.20).

He based his life's work on his claim that he had 'seen the Lord' like the other 'apostles' – and had been commissioned by him (1 Corinthians 9.1). But the evidence does not allow us to be sure about exactly how the dead Jesus was 'seen' to be alive, and to be 'Lord', by Paul or by anyone else. Was it seeing a person deeply loved who had seemed lost for ever but now stood there, in the flesh? Or was this an exceptionally influential instance of the psychic phenomena which are very often reported as the bereaved feel themselves to be in contact with the dead? Or was the appearance of the risen Lord an event in 'virtual reality', to be compared with an image on a screen, or a voice on a phone, communicating the power of a person who is not physically present? In the Acts of the Apostles (less significantly than in the words of Paul himself) it is said that those around him 'heard the voice but could see no one' (9.7), and that he saw the light but it was a 'vision' (26.19). I want to set out the other evidence carefully (although in this limited space I must now suspend my practice of giving exact biblical references).

A list of 'appearances' given to the Corinthians in his first letter (chapter 15) is a reminder of a 'tradition' which Paul had 'received' and had already 'handed on' to them. The list begins by saying that Jesus was buried and 'raised to life on the third day' but does not explicitly mention an empty tomb. It says that Jesus 'appeared to

Cephas' (Peter), to 'the Twelve' and to 'more than five hundred of the brothers at once, most of whom are still alive'. Only three other appearances are mentioned by Paul – to James the brother of Jesus, to 'all the apostles' (special envoys), and 'last of all to me; it was like a sudden, abnormal birth' because Paul had been persecuting the Christians. No details are given, presumably because the Christians in Corinth did not dispute that Christ had been raised from the dead; what worried some of them was whether they would be.

The gospels, all written later than Paul's letters, do not agree totally with his list of appearances, give different accounts of the appearances which they do relate, and do not describe the resurrection itself. The fourth gospel says that the first appearance was to the heartbroken Mary of Magdala, although Paul includes no woman in his list. There is no account of the appearance to Peter 'on the third day', although according to Paul this was the first indication that the crucified Jesus was alive and 'Lord'. Nor is there any mention of the appearance to James, whose role in the leadership of the early Christians was to be approximately as important as Peter's or Paul's. Nor is there any narrative of the appearance to the 500, which if accepted as an event would be specially impressive.

The earliest surviving copies of Mark's gospel say that a 'young man' (presumably believed to be an angel) told three women inside the empty tomb of Jesus that 'he has been raised' and would show himself to his disciples in Galilee 'but they told nothing to anyone, for they were afraid' – and there these copies end. Matthew's gospel relates that an earthquake had already opened the graves of many 'saints' who walked into Jerusalem, and that after the resurrection of Jesus and another earthquake an angel rolled away the stone which had guarded the entrance to his tomb. The appearance of this angel caused the terrified guards to fall to the ground but he gave the same message as in Mark to two women who were also present. Then Jesus himself appeared 'suddenly' and the women clasped his feet. Afterwards Jesus appeared as promised to the Eleven in Galilee. Luke's gospel tells of some women who found the stone already rolled away but were asked by 'two men in dazzling garments': 'Why search among the dead for one who is alive?' Later that day Jesus walked with two disciples on the road to Emmaus and had a long conversation with them about his mission but was not recognized until supper that evening, before vanishing. Luke also tells of appearances to Peter (not described) and to 'the rest of the company' (including at a meal) followed by a walk culminating in another disappearance. In the Acts of the Apostles he tells of 40 days over which Jesus 'ate and drank' with the apostles before 'a cloud took him from their sight', an ascension which is to be followed one day in the future by a return from the sky. The fourth gospel adds two appearances to 'the disciples' in a locked room in Jerusalem, and one appearance to seven of them including Peter on a shore by the lake of Galilee.

These references to the appearances cannot be harmonized as to names, dates and places. It has been claimed that the differences are no more than are to be expected from different witnesses, but the disagreements and improbabilities are such that no court of law would be satisfied by such evidence, then or now. (Mark says that when Jesus was examined before his crucifixion the witnesses against him were found unconvincing because 'their statements did not tally'.) It is easy for those of us who love the Easter stories to forget the questions likely to occur to any intelligent modern person hearing them for the first time. If the body of Jesus dematerialized, why was Jerusalem not destroyed by a nuclear explosion? If his risen body was clothed in normal dress, where did the clothes come from? Can we trust reports that the tomb was found to be empty when the evidence about it comes only from Christians and dates from between 30 and 60 years after the event? Is it not possible that the body of Jesus was thrown away? Every one of the Easter stories leaves the impression that those who first encountered the empty tomb and the risen Jesus were astonished and bewildered, so it ought not to seem surprising that in our own time questions are asked.

What seems certain is that the decision about the tomb's emptiness and the risen Lord's physicality must depend on wider belief or unbelief; before we can decide about this claim, we must have decided how far we can trust the early Christians to be accurately factual, and how far we can find room in what we believe about God for a miracle removing or transforming this dead body. Those who find the answers very easy may be invited to remember that according to the gospels this was the greatest miracle ever, never observed but beginning what Paul called a 'new creation'. Modern-minded believers who accept it can compare it only with the unimaginable singularity at the beginning of the creation of the universe.

It also seems certain that the Easter stories should not be treated like a modern detective story. It was not that everyone then was gullible, for we know that the Christians' claim about the resurrection was laughed at by Jews and Gentiles alike, but in defence of their faith the Christians evidently felt no need to assemble an account of the events which would be undeniably accurate, with every clue leading to a conviction about the empty tomb. One reason was that no great interest was then taken in accuracy by historians; the crucial story of Paul's conversion is told three times in the Acts of the Apostles, but each time with different details. But the main reason was that being sure about the details of the Easter event was not what made the Christians Christian. Paul told the Christians in Corinth bluntly that 'if Christ was not raised, then our gospel is null and void, and so too is your faith'. However, his gospel and their faith did not concern the literal accuracy of the Easter narratives in the gospels, which were not yet written. It concerned appearances of Jesus when he had been 'raised to life', from which Christians should derive the hope that those in their fellowship who have already died are not 'utterly lost' and that they themselves will be raised in spiritual bodies – as we might say, in personal identities – which will be imperishable and glorious, not of 'flesh and blood' made of 'dust'.

Like the rest of us, Paul could not imagine Jesus being alive eternally without imagining what he called his 'body of glory' when writing to the Philippians, but it seems highly probable that he did not believe in the flesh-and-blood, fish-eating body which appears in the gospels of Luke and John. Any such stories would not have fascinated him: when writing to the Galatians he recalled that after his conversion he had waited for three years before going to Jerusalem to ask for information from Peter and James – and he added 'God knows I am not lying!' The resurrection of Jesus meant everything to him, but its details did not. As he told the Galatians, what changed him was a revelation 'in' him and that was what began his mission 'in the peoples' – within the world of the Gentiles.

*   *   *

Paul's attitude to the question about Easter can, I believe, be connected with his attitude to the question about Judaism. He had been scandalized by Stephen's leadership of a group of Greek-speaking Jews who claimed that the work of Jesus had made the Jerusalem temple redundant, and he had 'savagely' tried to destroy the little Christian movement. But having been deeply shaken by the Jesus movement (as the intensity of his reaction shows), he now called it 'the Church of God' and led its outreach to the Gentiles. He insisted that male Gentiles need not be circumcised like Jews and should be welcomed to full fellowship with Jewish Christians, although they need not obey the Jewish food laws. The battleground was not now the centrality of the temple: many Jews lived far from Jerusalem and their religion was to continue when the temple had been demolished. The battle was over the most sensitive part of a man's body – and over almost every meal. In a confrontation in Antioch over these issues he attacked Peter and defied James, who now led the Christian community in Jerusalem.

It was not that he thought all Jews hypocritical or devoid of a sense of God's mercy: he had been a very devout Pharisee himself, leading a life which he could recall as 'faultless', and he knew perfectly well that devout Jews depended on God's 'grace'. His objection was to the attitude that obedience to the Jewish religious law automatically earned God's favour and lifted one to a level which made fellowship with Gentiles impossible. By taking this stand he made Christianity more than a movement within Judaism – and he began the Christian tradition of arguing about the significance of Jesus as 'Christ'.

Through the Greek *Christos* the word translates the Hebrew *Messiah*, the 'Anointed', the king whose triumph would recall the days of King David. In Paul's letter to Rome and in the Acts of the Apostles it is said that *Iesous* (the Greek version of the Hebrew *Yeshu*) was declared by God to be Messiah through his resurrection. The fourth gospel says that Andrew told Peter that he had 'found Messiah' before Peter met Jesus and that soon Jesus was telling a Samaritan woman who he was, and was demanding that 'the Jews' should acknowledge him. Mark's gospel says that Peter eventually recognized the Messiahship and that Jesus did not disclaim it, but that the plain 'I am' was delayed until Jesus was directly questioned by the high priest. Matthew and Luke, however, report a more guarded reply in their account of this examination at which no Christian was present. In view of this complicated evidence, many scholars have doubted whether Jesus ever actually claimed to be Messiah. Certainly he refused to fulfil the role of military hero: instead of leading a revolt against the Romans, he urged turning the other cheek and going the second mile when tough Jewish men were insulted by soldiers and forced to carry their heavy packs.

Yet he announced that the longed-for 'age to come' had arrived with him and that to him was the all-important function of Messiah as God's prime minister. So Paul was able to detach *Christos* from its political and military background and use it almost as the surname of Jesus as he took the proclamation of the new age to Jew and Gentile alike. He did not find it easy to reach the position that now 'there is no such thing as Jew and Greek, slave and free, man and woman, for you are all one person in Christ'. In many ways he never left the Jewish tradition. The opening of his letter to Rome flames with a Jew's indignation against the idolatry and immorality which were flaunted in that city. Before the letter ends he has been eloquent about his pride in his people: 'theirs is the glory of the divine presence, theirs the covenants, the law, the worship in the temple, the promises'. He could say that the purpose of his mission to the Gentiles was to provoke his fellow Jews to envy – yet he did turn to the Gentiles, changing the history of the world.

He did not start a new religion. He tried to 'imitate Christ' because he saw 'the glory of God in the face of Jesus Christ', not in his own mirror, and his essential creed was 'Jesus is Lord'. We know that he wrestled to find the meaning of his Lord's apparently scandalous death and we can guess that he often spoke about the life of the man who had given crucifixion this wealth of significance. He carefully communicated what he had been told about the Last Supper as well as about the number of the appearances after the resurrection, and he referred to the teaching of Jesus when discussing divorce or the right of the apostles not to depend on ordinary jobs. He held up Jesus as the supreme example of humility and love and quoted key words in the Aramaic language spoken by Jesus: *Abba* ('Father!') and *Marana tha* ('Lord, come!').

What he could not quote was any clear command by Jesus before his death that the mission must be taken to the Gentiles without turning the Gentiles into Jews – because there had been no such command. Yet Paul was convinced that Jesus had commissioned him for this mission and that this acutely controversial development was necessary, because of the purpose of God that 'in Christ all will be brought to life'. He told the Christians in Rome that 'once the Gentiles have been admitted in full strength, the whole of Israel will be saved . . . In shutting up all humankind in the prison of their disobedience, God's purpose was to show mercy to all.' That letter is among his writings which show that he was often despondent: most of the Jews had rejected Jesus and few Gentiles had accepted him.

Yet he kept his vision of the unconquerable mission about Jesus to all. James Dunn presented this vision with unsurpassed scholarship in *The Theology of Paul the Apostle* (1998).

It seems to follow that if he had been addressing the modern situation, Paul would have understood the mission of God about Jesus to 'all' as including 'all' in lands traditionally non-Christian and in lands with a Christian past but a modern present. As Paul once interpreted the good news in terms which Gentiles could understand, so the message must now be given not only within Asian spirituality (for example) but also within the modern world of science-based thought. For everybody, in any generation or culture, a deeply felt and believed Christianity must mean that 'Christ' is revealed 'in me', as Christ was in Paul – and revealed within a person's own culture, as Paul's message about Christ was spread 'in the peoples'. The jigsaw puzzle of the personality of Jesus must be assembled inside the person confronted by it, until that person finds that the puzzle is intelligible 'for me', and 'in me' the Lord is risen indeed.

In our age many Christians will continue to believe in the general reliability of the witness to the resurrection of Jesus given in the New Testament, and that for them is the Easter faith, but it seems to me and to many others that what is essential in 'belief in the resurrection' is simply this. After the death of Jesus very strange events occurred which transformed the lives of his closest followers, healed their memories and awakened both faith and imagination. Other events have occurred since then which have made believers say, with Paul, that Christ 'once took hold of me'. We, too, have felt that he walks mysteriously with us through life, and meets us when we are in tears, or have locked ourselves in, or when we go about our business – and he commands us to 'follow me'.

*   *   *

Paul believed that the reality which he had met in the dead-but-alive, crucified-but-crowned Christ had not begun with a human birth. We can know this whether it was Paul or a disciple of his who wrote to the Colossians about Christ that he is 'the image of the invisible God' because 'in him God in all his fullness chose to dwell'. In his first letter to Corinth Paul taught that all things exist 'through' Christ although 'there is one God'. He did not pause to explain this but most scholars think that in the background is the Jewish belief that God created everything through his 'wisdom'. This vision of Christ as the human name of the divine wisdom was close to the prologue of the fourth gospel, where it is said that 'all things came to be' through the divine 'Word', Speech or Reason (*Logos*) which became 'flesh' in Jesus. It is also close to the prologue to the Letter to Hebrews, where it is said that through the 'Son' God both 'created the worlds' and 'has spoken to us'.

However, in these parts of the New Testament it is not claimed that the birth of Jesus was physically unusual. Paul does not name Joseph or Mary; he says simply that Jesus was descended from King David and was 'born of a woman'. The stories that Jesus was conceived without intercourse between his parents are found only in the gospels of Matthew and Luke. It seems obvious that both gospels include legends: Matthew tells of astrologers who were guided by a star which stopped 'above the place where the child lay' and who left behind very expensive gifts although the family remained poor, and Luke recounts a series of marvels involving angels who speak or sing, although in Mark's earlier gospel the mother, brothers and sisters of Jesus think him crazy when he begins to preach.

In the time when Matthew and Luke wrote, it was believed that the mother's body was no more than the earth in which the man's seed could be planted, so that it seemed appropriate to believe also that in the conception of Jesus the seed was somehow planted by the Spirit of God. Later there was more awareness of the mother's role but also of the sinfulness of humanity, so that it seemed appropriate to add the belief that Mary was 'immaculate' because sinless from her own conception. But it seems to many Christians in our own time perfectly adequate to think that the Holy Spirit – the Divine Energy – was powerfully at work in all that led up to the birth of Jesus, including the sexual love of Joseph and Mary expressed naturally. Indeed, this seems necessary if it is to be believed that Jesus was genuinely human, as were his father and mother. It is relevant that when the prologue to the fourth gospel speaks of birth 'not of human stock, by the physical desire of a human father', the reference is not to the unique manner of the conception of Jesus: it is a description of all who have accepted Jesus and have put their trust in him after the activity of the Spirit in their hearts.

Belief in the virginal conception of Jesus as a literal fact has often been valued by Christians as a support for faith in Jesus as 'God the Son' but it is possible to believe in that miracle without drawing that conclusion from it: the Quran teaches both that Jesus had no human father and that he was a great prophet, but no more than that. Modern discussion has made it clear that the unique relationship between Jesus and 'the Father' does not depend on the manner of his birth being unique. It depends on the evidence that Jesus had an extraordinary sense that he totally depended on the Father and was full of the Father's power – a sense of dependence and power that he has been able to communicate to countless people. The response to this evidence has been expressed in a creed by saying that Jesus 'came down from heaven' having been 'begotten of his Father before all worlds'. But it is not necessary to take either metaphor literally.

Nor is it necessary to insist that as a matter of fact Jesus was born in Bethlehem, not Nazareth. Although Matthew's gospel says that his parents lived there but settled in Nazareth some years after his birth, Luke evidently found the connection with Nazareth so strong that he has to account for a visit to Bethlehem by a story about a census of the Roman Empire for which there is no other evidence (although there was a local census when the Romans took over direct rule in Judaea in AD 6). In John's gospel Nathanael is told about 'Jesus, son of Joseph, from Nazareth' and asks 'Can anything good come from Nazareth?' – a reference to that obscure Galilean village which shows why King David's home village in Judaea would have been thought more suitable than Nazareth for the birth of Messiah as 'Son of David'.

Of course I appreciate that for many millions of people, church-goers or not, reasoning about 'what probably happened' is not something to be done at Christmas and of course I do not propose the abolition of the Christmas stories or the Christmas music. People love Christmas. So do I: the great Christmas tree outside St Martin-in-the-Fields still shines for me, I still hear the boy singing 'Once in Royal David's City' to the world from Cambridge, for 40 years I have celebrated Christmas as a priest in other great churches. But it seems important to let it be known that intelligent Christians can tell the difference between a great story and a down-to-earth fact. Otherwise the faith that God came down to earth in the thoroughly human life of Jesus is likely to be thought to be in the same class as the story of Father Christmas. And I feel the same about the gospels which have moved me, and many worshipping with me, at many Easters.

In 1986, after controversies surrounding Bishop David Jenkins, the Church of England's House of Bishops issued a document on *The Nature of Christian Belief* with a wise refusal to allow a trial for heresy ('such proceedings do more harm than good') combined with a pastoral sensitivity to the indignation about some provocative phrases used by the bishop – both before this eirenic report and after it. But there is no need to be as cautiously diplomatic as most of the bishops.

They agreed corporately to 'uphold' belief in the Empty Tomb and the Virgin Birth as 'expressing' the faith of the Church, seeing the first as 'affirming that in the resurrection life the material order is redeemed and the fullness of human nature, bodily, mental and spiritual, is glorified for eternity' – and the second as affirming that 'in Christ God has taken the initiative for our salvation by uniting with himself our human nature, so bringing to birth a new humanity'. Yet they added that their own views were 'divergent' about the Empty Tomb: 'scholarship can offer no conclusive demonstration' and 'no one could ever hope to observe or describe the working of such a miracle'. They were also 'divergent' about the Virgin Birth or Virginal Conception: it is a question 'whether or not it is to be regarded as an historical fact' and 'a critical weighing of New Testament indications is bound to be an inconclusive and even marginal exercise'. So it is impossible to be sure about what exactly was meant by corporately upholding the traditional beliefs – and it does not seem that they should be upheld as essential to Christian belief today or tomorrow.

*   *   *

Although there may well be historical truth in the story of the keen interest taken by Jesus in the temple during a pilgrimage to Jerusalem when he was 12 years old, what is known to history begins where Mark's gospel begins – with John the Baptist and with Jesus the Baptized.

There is plenty of evidence about the work of the Baptist, a stern preacher in the tradition of the prophets, calling on the Jews to repent and to be cleansed spiritually through immersion in death-like water. He predicted imminent doom for those who did not heed the call. There is nothing unlikely in the reports that Yeshu the carpenter of Nazareth was one of those who responded totally. His name meant 'God saves' and the time of salvation had come: he was himself baptized and he joined the Baptist's mission. His own followers would not have been likely to tell such a story in the belief that it honoured their Lord. On the contrary, the facts were awkward: their Lord had been baptized among sinners and had joined, not led, the mission. So in Matthew's gospel the Baptist says that he needs to be baptized by Jesus, and in Luke's he does homage to Jesus (his cousin) while still in his mother's womb.

In the history of Christianity much attention has been paid to preachers and leaders who have been as severe as the Baptist, and the response of Jesus to him illustrates that this kind of holiness can make a transforming impact in minds that are open. Mark's gospel, however, states near its own beginning the far more positive message which Jesus was to spread: 'After John had been arrested, Jesus came into Galilee proclaiming the good news of God: the time has arrived, the kingdom of God is upon you.' A little later in this gospel Jesus promises: 'there are some standing here who will not taste death until they see that the kingdom of God has come with power'. As Matthew and Luke agree, the essential and thrilling message of Jesus was that God reigns and that his rule on earth as in heaven is about to be brought about by God. In the Baptist's message this prospect had been bad news for most people. For Jesus too, this was a warning – but chiefly it was a promise, like an invitation to a banquet. The Baptist may have been influenced by the Essenes whose monastery in the desert at Qumran was not far from his headquarters by the river Jordan; they also demanded purity, bathed often, seeking it for themselves, and expected a rapid intervention by God in decisive judgement. (Their Dead Sea Scrolls were rediscovered in caves, in the 1940s and later.) But Jesus befriended and taught people where they were, physically and morally, and his message was one which they could understand with excitement and welcome with joy: the judgement predicted by the Baptist had been postponed so as to give time for repentance. Life around Jesus was now like children making a game out of weddings; life around the Baptist had been like children playing at funerals.

What did Jesus teach and do during this mission? It was something uniquely his own. Matthew's gospel reflects this in the report that the Baptist was as puzzled as anyone has ever been, sending messages to ask Jesus what was going on. The rabbis taught by argument about exactly what the Scriptures implied, but Matthew presents Jesus as the innovator ('but I say to you . . .') and what seems to have been an unusual habit of his is preserved, beginning

what he is to teach with 'Amen, Amen' ('In truth, in very truth . . .').
And while the Scriptures were believed to condemn many ways of
sinning or becoming impure, and to demand a solemn act to express
repentance, it is reported that Jesus – neither a trained rabbi nor a
priest of the temple – seemed shockingly quick to tell people 'your
sins are forgiven'.

He is mentioned by the Roman historians Tacitus and Suetonius
and by the Jewish historian Josephus, and some sayings which seem
authentic are preserved in early Christian sources not included in the
New Testament, but our only hope of gaining much information
must rest on the gospels which were made 'canonical' by inclusion.
It has of course very often been noticed that these are four different
gospels and it is now no secret that most modern scholars agree that
they were all written not by eye-witnesses or by neutral historians
but by fervent believers some time after the crucifixion. These are
not memories always arranged in the order in which the events took
place. On the contrary, they are narratives which may be compared
with pearls on a string, the pearls having been fished up by the
editor/author from an ocean of early Christian story-telling and
preaching. It is striking how much of the setting in Palestine in or
around AD 30 has been preserved but we have always to remember
that these are not tape-recordings: here we see Jesus through the eyes
of Christians of the first century, as we meet him through Christian
lives in the present day. So it would appear that originally there was
no intention to insist on a single, authoritative account of what Jesus
was and is.

The gospel in which this strange style of writing was first used is
almost certainly the one attributed to Mark (although none of the
four carries the name of its author). It has been well described as a
gospel for martyrs and that description is apt whether or not it was
written by the John Mark who was a personal assistant to Paul and
later to Peter, as was related in an early tradition. It seems to have
been written not long after the martyrdoms of Peter and Paul, which
probably occurred during the persecution under Nero in AD 64, but
it is certainly not propaganda for the apostles. All the attention is on
the central figure, who is obviously challenging but also, if we look
closer, attractive.

Here Jesus fascinates but the scene is one of human weakness. His
closest disciples do not understand him and are stupidly ambitious
for themselves; in the end one of them betrays him to the police. His

enemies are an extraordinary coalition, united by him: the puritani-
cal Pharisees in Galilee, Herod Antipas the local ruler who was no
Puritan, the aristocratic priests in Jerusalem, the Roman governor.
His own family thinks that he is out of his mind; he cannot achieve
healings in his own sceptical village; when he can be a healer, he gets
so tired that he sleeps during a storm on the lake; he faces the
prospect of death in 'horror and anguish'; he declares that 'no one is
good except God alone' but as he dies he shouts that God has abandoned him. He warns those who follow him that only if they 'lose'
life will they 'save' it. Each must be ready to drink the cup of suffering; for each there will be a cross.

It is not immediately clear why Mark calls this grim story good
news about 'Jesus Christ the Son of God'. It ends with women who
have been told to spread the news of the resurrection saying 'nothing
to anyone, for they were afraid'. And yet if we look carefully we can
see why such a gospel could appeal so widely (although gradually) in
the Roman Empire. Here Jesus pronounces the forgiveness of sins
without waiting for any ritual purification or sacrifice. He heals
people without waiting for the sacred day of rest to end. He teaches
that pollution is caused by what comes out of a mouth, not by what
goes into it. He visits a heavily polluted neighbourhood, among
tombs and pigs. He denounces commerce in the temple's Court of
the Gentiles. He reaches out to the margins of society, healing a
woman made 'unclean' for 12 years, responding to a foreigner
whose small daughter is ill, rebuking disciples who try to chase children away while he teaches. Jesus of Mark is not a grim fanatic. For
such a Lord, a martyr could be willing.

Matthew's gospel appears to have come out of a crisis almost as
painful as the imminent prospect of martyrdom – the crisis of the
split between the little churches and the synagogues. It may have
been written in Antioch, where Peter may have been based before his
move to Rome; here Peter is highly honoured. In the background is a
church struggling to preserve unity between Jew and Gentile in its
membership, now as in the time of the confrontation between Peter
and Paul; this is the only gospel to use the word translated as
'church' (*ekklesia*). It involves high praise for the Christian who,
although he has found new treasures, remains a Jew, 'keeps the law
and teaches others to do so'. But it also includes attacks on Jews
who are enemies, on Pharisees ('hypocrites') and rabbis ('blind
guides'). Through this gospel the cry of a Jewish crowd which

demands the death of Jesus, 'his blood be on us and our children', has echoed down the centuries with terrible consequences as Christians have persecuted Jews. It is a gospel where emotions are raw, and these emotions include hatred.

Such a gospel has some historical roots further back, in the actual conflicts between Jesus the Jew and the Jewish religious leadership, but plainly Jesus had not been an anti-semite. And Matthew, who was almost certainly a Jew himself, has collected sayings about the life of Christian discipleship to make the Sermon on the Mount, and here Jesus unambiguously condemns all hatred. In this extremely provocative sermon anger is as bad as murder and a lustful look is as bad as adultery, and enemies must be loved with a love like God's. Standards are set which must challenge even the most sensitive conscience: the truth must be spoken so consistently that oaths are never needed, anyone who asks for a loan or a gift must be given one, almsgiving and prayer must be practised secretly, people must be perfect themselves and not critics of anyone else. But even those standards are good news, because in comparison with them, all fail: all are sinners and none should feel excluded from the kingdom of God by a sinful past. Positively, these are glimpses of what life could be like in that kingdom, inspired by a love for the Father who is both truly perfect and infinitely compassionate. For everyday life these are challenges, not regulations. So this carpenter can claim that, in contrast with the yoke and burden of the detailed Jewish religious law, 'my yoke is easy and my burden light'. And so the Sermon on the Mount has itself been a mountain towering over the confused emotions, and over the day-by-day practicalities and compromises, of Christian life through 20 centuries.

Luke's gospel shows the appeal of Jesus to the ancient world – and to moderns – still more clearly. It begins with great predictions: 'dawn from on high' is breaking and filling the world with light and glory. It continues with a sense that victory can already be celebrated: Jesus tells his disciples that he has 'watched Satan fall from heaven like a flash of lightning'. It ends with the expansion of the Church 'beginning in Jerusalem' – and the second volume, the Acts of the Apostles, ends with Paul in Rome. The author may have been the physician called Luke who is mentioned by Paul as a companion, and the 'we' passages in Acts point in that direction – but he was also a great story-teller, retelling the short stories of Jesus with a very rare skill and also including passages about Paul which cannot be reconciled with Paul's own letters. Probably a Gentile himself, he was excited by a mission to the marginalized which was also a mission to the world. More than a third of this gospel is special to him and here the attitude of Jesus to non-Jews is always positive.

This attitude brings about the rapid rejection of Jesus by his own village, but near the end the Roman governor is convinced that he is innocent. In the middle come stories where a Samaritan shows a Jew what it means to be a good neighbour and a father runs towards a son returning from life among the pigs in the Gentile world while the righteous elder brother (Israel) sulks.

The Jesus of Luke is also extraordinary in his attitude to women. His heart goes out to widows and prostitutes alike; they are people with needs and he asks Simon the Pharisee 'do you *see* this woman?' He is delighted when women want to listen to his teaching, and to express their love emotionally, and in return he and his male disciples are accompanied and financed by a group of well-off women. Women are near to him even while he is being crucified. And the Jesus of Luke identifies himself with the poor. His parables show a great sensitivity to a woman who is desperate because she cannot get justice and to a housewife who is frantic because she cannot find a coin. The rich are fools who are warned about hell.

The material which is common to Matthew and Luke presents Jesus as announcing a banquet to which Gentiles will come 'from east and west, from north and south'. He is a countryman who loves the glory of wild flowers yet is convinced that what is now being done by God through him is greater than the glory of King Solomon. He is himself homeless like foxes or birds, yet he alone knows 'who the Father is'. He brings sharp divisions but those who reject him reject God. He calls at least some of his disciples to leave their families because the mission is urgent and the time will be short, but emphatically it is a mission with good news: the truly happy are the poor, the hungry, the mourners and the unpopular, because as God establishes his rule on earth they will be fully consoled and meanwhile they can trust that God will provide all that they really need. God is like a father who gives a child a loaf, not a stone; a fish, not a snake; an egg, not a scorpion. The prayer which Jesus gives for his disciples to recite sums everything up – and does not include much which has preoccupied the churches. It addresses the Eternal as *Abba*, 'Father', yet God is a uniquely holy mystery. It puts first the coming of the Father's kingdom on earth and it trusts him to supply daily needs. It asks for forgiveness and offers it to all. It acknowledges all human weakness and prays to be spared the unendurable.

*   *   *

These gospels do not say that Jesus was primarily a miracle-worker. Evidence has survived of others who worked wonders in Galilee; indeed they are mentioned in the gospels. In an age when doctors were few, primitive and expensive, there was a great call for people who would nowadays be called faith-healers, and stories about miracles changing nature were also believed quite easily. The question was not whether miracles occurred, but whether the power in them came from God or demons. It was assumed that evil events including sickness were caused by these evil spirits, and Jesus shared this belief; he is reported to have said that he threw out demons by the 'finger of God'. And we should not think that all these beliefs were strong only long ago: they are strong in many places in the world as the twenty-first century begins, and specially strong in the Pentecostal form of Christianity which to many millions now seems to be the form which means most. To many other Christians the ready acceptance of frequent miracles seems very strange – and yet one has to admit that such a faith can get results.

The stories of healing by Jesus never include a magician's spell; instead we get *Talitha cum* ('Little girl, get up!') or *Ephphatha* ('Open your mouth!'). They show Jesus responding when confronted by distress but not seeking publicity or making a career out of it. He exercises the power of God which is within him but, being human, feels the power going out of him. The healings depend on faith – always on his own faith, sometimes on the faith of people connected with the sufferer, more often on the arousal of the healing power of faith in the sick who would otherwise interpret their illness as demon-inflicted punishment by God for sin. Significant phrases are 'your sins are forgiven you' and 'your faith has healed you'. Some of the stories are easier to believe than others; for example, many of the sick called 'lepers' may have suffered from a skin disease with a psychosomatic cause, leading to an acute feeling of guilt and isolation. None of the stories needs to be completely accurate; for example, someone then believed to be dead may have been in a coma. None says whether the cure was permanent (much 'faith-healing' is not). And especially when they do not involve healing, miracle stories may be just that – stories.

Mark includes two stories about the multiplication of baked loaves and (cooked?) fishes, feeding either 4,000 or 5,000, in a legend which may have been based on a wonderfully impressive communal meal after hearing Jesus teach. A fig tree which is cursed and withered when it does not bear fruit out of season may have had roots in parables: people may be compared with unfruitful trees but leaves on a fig tree are a sign that 'summer is near' – despite human failures, the kingdom of God is coming. The story of walking on the water may have originated in a story about the risen (and weightless) Lord appearing to disciples near or on the lake. Such 'demythologizing' suggestions may seem shocking, but perhaps it is now more shocking when miracles are preached about to the modern-minded without any discussion of the question whether they really happened. This practice is shocking because it means that the modern-minded are discouraged from taking seriously the large parts of the gospels which are devoted to the more understandable celebration of Jesus the Healer.

*   *   *

The material common to Matthew and Luke does not include an account of the last days of Jesus before his death, and there are considerable differences between Mark and John, but the main facts are clear enough. A reconstruction which is exciting, and on the whole convincing, was provided by N. T. Wright's *Jesus and the Victory of God* (1996).

The crisis was not caused by a debate about ideas. There was then a very lively debate within Judaism about how *Torah* (Law) should be interpreted. The Pharisees who were to prevail when the temple and the nation had been destroyed were in dispute with the Sadducees who did not believe in any desirable kind of life after death but did believe in the maintenance of the temple, collaborating with the Romans for this purpose until shortly before the great rebellion of AD 66. The supporters of armed resistance to the Romans, later called Zealots, were in dispute with the Essenes who waited for military intervention by God; and the sterner Shammai and the more liberal Hillel were honoured by different groups as teachers of the religious law. All these movements had ideas about how best to hasten the promised time when the God of Israel would be acknowledged as king over Israel and over all the earth, and all these movements aired their differences within the bond provided by their ethnic identity. But Jesus was different. He announced that the kingdom of God was already beginning, in his own work and under his command – but did not call for a stricter purity in keeping laws or offering sacrifices, or for a rebellion, or for a monastery, or for a mere relaxation of the laws. He called for a new start, for a radically renewed Israel, for a new world where the power would be the power of love, divine and human. And the call was then very urgent because the clear alternative was the destruction of temple and nation in rebellion against Rome, followed by concentration on a race's survival, not on a mission to the world. According to Luke, on his way to his death Jesus told weeping women to mourn for themselves and their children.

He decided that he must go to Jerusalem during the crowded and tense festival which commemorated the liberation of Israel from slavery in Egypt. He, the Liberator appointed by the Father, must not remain in the comparative safety of Galilee. He must make a final challenge to the authorities and the people to accept the kingdom of God, and if he must die in the process Jerusalem is the traditional place for the rejection of God's messengers.

When he rode into the city it was on a donkey as a symbol of a peaceful mission, but when some voices hailed him as Messiah, he must have known what would be the reaction of the Romans and their collaborators. According to Luke the people around Jesus 'thought the kingdom of God might dawn at any moment' and according to Mark the demonstration on the first Palm Sunday was political, hailing 'the kingdom of our father David'. Instead of lying low, Jesus himself made a demonstration in the temple which was bound to infuriate the aristocratic priests in charge. Instead of retreating while there was time, he returned to teach openly and controversially. One of the inner circle of his disciples informed the priests where he could be arrested quietly. The motive of Judas 'son of Simon Iscariot' is not known certainly: he may have been a thief who was bribed as the early Christians believed, but Jesus (no fool) had trusted him, and since *sicarius* was the name given to a guerrilla or 'freedom fighter', and since it is reported that he soon committed suicide, it has been thought possible that he gambled and lost on the possibility of being able to force Jesus into leading a rebellion.

It has also been suggested (most famously by Albert Schweitzer) that Jesus was himself a gambler, accepting the risk of death in order to force his Father into the great, final miracle, the establishment of the kingdom of God – and dying in despair when the gamble failed. But it is far more probable that Jesus, who staked his whole life and work on obedience to the Father, prayed that he might be spared a dreadful death, before accepting it as the Father's will. The early Christians would not have been likely to invent the story of the agony in Gethsemane, where Jesus prayed 'with loud cries and tears' (says the Letter to Hebrews). This was a dark hour when his courage broke down temporarily, as his faith was to break down during the further agony of crucifixion with the apparently total failure of his life and work. But it seems clear that when calm he accepted that his death must come before the coming of the kingdom, and all the gospels say that he declared this plainly to his disciples at their last supper together. Deeply embedded in the traditions about him is the belief that he had already said that, despite his great hope and high expectation, he did not know the 'hour' when the kingdom would come or the form which it would take. The early Christians recorded that combination of expectation with ignorance, resulting in acute disappointment, although it would seem to make their Lord less than perfect. We may say that it showed that he was truly human. Certainly the early Christians did not think that because of it Jesus should be forgotten as a deluded optimist. Instead, they saw the drinking of the cup of suffering by their Lord as the essential prelude to that longed-for government by God, a government decisively inaugurated by the strange victory of the crucified.

It is also extremely unlikely that the early Christians invented the story of that last supper. It was a part of the tradition about which Paul reminded the Corinthians but it was not produced by a desire to imitate other cults: on the contrary, eating human 'flesh' and drinking human 'blood' were bound to lead to the rumour that the Christians were cannibals and were also bound to be a scandal to Jews forbidden to taste blood in meat. What seems certain is that Jesus implied that the sacrifices in the temple were about to have their fulfilment in his own sacrifice of himself. He also intended to assure his disciples that his physical death would not mean the end of his spiritual presence among them, but precisely how this presence is made real has often been argued about between Christians, and some disagreement about the significance of the Last Supper begins within the New Testament, being connected with a disagreement about the right date.

Mark, Matthew and Luke report that it was the Passover meal, carefully prepared as such, but John's gospel says that it was a supper eaten before the great festival. The three earlier gospels say that Jesus was arrested, tried and crucified during the festival but that his body could not be prepared for burial that evening because then the Sabbath began – and John does agree that the death was on a Friday. He tells us, however, that this year the Passover festival coincided with the Sabbath, meaning that Jesus died while the lambs were being sacrificed in the temple in preparation for the Passover supper. This disagreement about dates has had the result that scholars cannot agree about the year, which may have been 27, 30 or 33. John may have intended to make a theological point by changing the date previously agreed, but if so he makes the point only by mentioning that in accordance with the scriptural law about the Passover lambs none of the bones of Jesus was broken. The earlier gospels may have intended to stress that it was particularly wrong to try and crucify Jesus on the very day of the sacred festival, but if so they make their point only by telling the story of the release of a criminal in order to please the festive crowd. But the point about which all these evangelists are agreed is that Jesus sacrificed his life during a festival commemorating a liberation from slavery. It is the only point which really matters.

The details of the story of the Last Supper are also not reported fully and unanimously. The oldest tradition known to us, conveyed by Paul to the church in Corinth, does not include the statement by Jesus in the earliest gospel that he will never again drink wine 'until that day when I drink it new in the kingdom of God'. In three of the gospels there is disagreement about whether the cup was drunk before or during the meal (Paul says 'after'), and eating the lamb is not recounted. In John's gospel wine is not mentioned and bread is given only to Judas. It seems clear that although the Last Supper was a fact, as were the birth and death, the New Testament does not enable us claim detailed knowledge as the foundation of detailed theology.

Mark, Matthew and Luke believed that Jesus was tried by the highest Jewish court, the high priest's council (the Sanhedrin), and sentenced to death because he blasphemously claimed to be Messiah, but this seems unlikely. A trial by night without reliable witnesses would be illegal; a claim to be Messiah, made by several rebels about this time, was not blasphemous; and although an enraged mob might stone someone to death and escape punishment, the formal power to inflict capital punishment was reserved to the local governor throughout the Roman Empire. It is more probable that Jesus was examined informally by the chief priests, refused to satisfy them about his orthodoxy, and was sent to Pilate as a dangerous troublemaker. Pilate had a reputation for cruelty excessive even by Roman standards and was to be recalled to Rome in AD 36. He may well have been mystified and even impressed by Jesus, but he could not afford to give him the benefit of any doubt. A Roman colonial governor trying an agitator who did not deny enthusiasm about a 'kingdom' other than Caesar's would not hesitate for long. So this 'King of the Jews' suffered the usual punishment. He was executed in an abandoned quarry just outside the city wall.

I am writing this during a crisis which was brought to a climax by one man's controversial visit to the site of the temple in Jerusalem – this time, however, a visit calculated to stir up hatreds. It is a time when the modern state of Israel, established as a homeland after the Holocaust, is extending its power into other people's territory – as the Romans did in the time of Jesus. And it is a time when some young Palestinians, unconsciously in the tradition of the rebels who defied Rome, see no alternative to becoming martyrs in order to convey a message – but in making that sacrifice they kill many civilians by bombs strapped to their own bodies. So the true cross can still be found in Jerusalem; it is a place of injustice, hatred, violence, grief and despair now, as when in Mark's picture 'darkness came over the whole land'.

*   *   *

One of the ways in which the fourth gospel differs from the other three is that it sees Jesus as knowing everything and moving through life and death without a flicker of doubt that he and the Father are 'one' – and he demands acknowledgement of who he is in quite long speeches. And there are other differences. This gospel says that within a week of his baptism Jesus performed the spectacular miracle of turning water into wine, and that not long afterwards he made his public demonstration in the temple in Jerusalem. These are followed by other great 'signs' of the glory which Jesus had 'with the Father before the world was'. He heals sickness without being physically present; he ends paralysis because 'those who hear shall come to life'; he makes the blind see and those who think they 'see' spiritually blind; he feeds a multitude in order to show that he is himself the 'bread of life'; he raises Lazarus from his tomb because he is 'the resurrection and the life'. In his speeches Jesus openly declares that he is the Son of Man 'who came down from heaven', Messiah, the Son of God, the light of the world, the eternal 'I am'. In his farewell speech and prayer he assures the disciples who are his 'friends' that he makes them clean and loving, peaceful and glad; he prepares heaven for them; he promises that on earth they will do mightier works than his, and that he will send 'the Spirit of truth' to stay with them for ever; he shares with them the glory which the Father gave him; he has conquered the world. He says that their love for each other must be as great as his love for them and he prays that their unity with each other may be as close as his union with the Father.

This gospel contains some material which is historically reliable, but it is equally certain that not all these deeds were done, and not all these words were spoken, by the historical Jesus, because they cannot be fitted into the gospels written earlier. To an extent they resemble the exhortations in the Revelation of John addressed by the Living One to the seven small but problem-filled churches under pressure in the Roman Empire's province of Asia – or the 114 sayings attributed to Jesus in the 'Gospel of Thomas' rediscovered in 1945, a document which seems to reflect mainly the mysticism of the movement known as the Gnostics (the 'Knowers'). The language is much the same here as in the three Letters of John addressed by an 'elder' to a small community around AD 90. And it is a relief to be able to see some distance between this fourth gospel and the historical Jesus, for it obscures some realities: his vulnerable humanity, his love of his fellow Jews (denounced at John 8.44 as 'children of the Devil'), his commandment to love neighbours as well as fellow disciples, his sense of humour, the agony in his faith.

Although this gospel was soon attributed to John the son of Zebedee, the incidents in which that apostle was most clearly involved according to the other gospels are not recounted here, and this gospel itself only claims that the tradition in it goes back to a disciple who is not named and who first appears in the narrative placed next to the Lord because he was the one whom 'Jesus loved' most. But the gospel also says that 'we' (also not named) 'know' that the witness of this beloved disciple is 'true'. It seems that the group behind the gospel, the 'we', is the one addressed in the Letters of John – a community which believes that it has passed 'from death to life' because it has obeyed the commands to love Jesus and 'one another'. As in the letters of Paul, we are given glimpses of the intense spiritual life of the early Christians. It seems both possible and right to use this portrait of Jesus by a saint with a deep insight very gratefully without claiming accuracy for parts of it which are contrary to the evidence provided by the earlier gospels. The phrase 'Jesus says' may often be right when this gospel is read in church, for we are entitled to believe that the saint did hear from the eternal Christ, but 'Jesus said' has often been used to support doctrines developed by Christians and that tradition deserves revision by those who, partly because they love this gospel, care about truth.

*   *   *

Early in this gospel (4.45) Samaritans converted by the woman with whom Jesus talked at Jacob's Well are convinced that he is 'the Saviour of the world'. The title 'Saviour', used about God or Jesus, is prominent in other documents written towards the end of Bible-writing, and in the Acts of the Apostles (4.12) Peter is represented as telling the Jewish 'rulers and elders' that 'there is no salvation through anyone else; in all the world no other name has been granted to humankind by which we can be saved'. No one who has ever had a deep experience of Christian conversion, or who has really belonged to a Christian congregation full of the spiritual presence of Jesus, can be surprised that such things have been said, and still are said, by Christians all over the world. Jesus Christ has had an effect on Christians which is absolutely unique in the history of religion, where no other human teacher has been regarded as 'Saviour' in a sense remotely like this; as Prophet yes, as Enlightened yes, but not a 'Saviour' in whom to trust for life and death, as 'God' may be trusted in other religions. But it does not follow that only Christians can be saved.

That has often been said by Christians, and has had the good result that a message about the Saviour has been taken to new groups and peoples with great courage, making the Church world-wide – but knowledge about the size of the world's population, and the goodness of many non-Christians in it, has gradually made it incredible that a loving Creator should exclude the vast majority of his human creation from salvation because that is a Christian monopoly.

Nor have solutions to the problem offered in the churches always seemed believable. It has been suggested that while non-Christian goodness will be rewarded, at best non-Christian worship will be overlooked or forgiven – but since the religion often inspires the good conduct, that seems illogical. (For the British this is not a distant problem: the Muslims now living in Britain have about 900 mosques. The population also includes about 400,000 Hindus and about the same number of Sikhs.) It has also been suggested that while those who respond to the Gospel are saved, those who reject it are damned. God's mercy will cover those who have never had an opportunity to respond – but still questions must arise. How often is the Gospel presented so worthily – in Bombay or in Birmingham – that people who watch or hear the Christians deserve to be damned eternally if they do not accept what the Christians say? And if God does make eternity depend on how people respond to Christians, why has the Christian Church not been inspired to be more energetic and convincing in evangelism? Can it really be the case that the sins of Christians cause people to be damned who would never have been excluded from salvation if they had never heard about Christianity?

As the size of the problem has been appreciated, it has seemed to many Christians inadequate to be merely negative or agnostic about God's plan for the vast majority of the human race: that does not sound like good news for the world. A large discussion has therefore developed about what it can mean to witness to Christ as 'the Saviour of the world' while not adding that the non-Christian world cannot be saved. It has been suggested that Christ's self-sacrifice enabled the Father to cease to be wrathful towards the world, but there is no evidence that Jesus taught this. It has been said that the cross changed the status of the world without the world being aware of it, but Jesus did teach emphatically that people (not the Father) must change in order to enter the kingdom of God. Non-Christians have been called anonymous Christians, but what is intended to be a compliment is rightly resented because it does not take their identity seriously enough (Christians would not like being called anonymous Muslims or Buddhists). Non-Christian religions and ethical traditions have been called the work of Christ, but that claim has no clear meaning unless the word 'Christ' is attached to a reality very much larger than the historical Jesus.

It seems far more promising to explore the idea that the divine work of creation, salvation and inspiration covers the whole human race: as is said in the prologue to the fourth gospel, the life brought by God's 'word' has been life and light for the whole of humankind, and the darkness has never overcome it. This divine work uses all that is good in history, including the world's religions, but its character is best revealed by Jesus. As the fourth gospel also teaches (14.6) he is the true way to God and no one 'comes to the Father' except through him, in the sense (we may say) that only he teaches and embodies the father-like love of God to the extent that is seen in past and present experience of him. His own parables gives us a clue to which sufficient attention has not been paid: they repeatedly praise what is good in the daily behaviour of the Jews around him, but the point is always that what Jesus brings is something new and unique. It would be a tragedy if, as its encounters with other religions develop, Christianity were to deny the goodness in almost all the children of the Father of all – but it would also be a tragedy if Christianity were to obscure the uniqueness of what is given in Jesus who offers himself as the Saviour of all.

*   *   *

It is very striking that the Christian community known to Matthew (28.19) baptized people 'in the name of the Father and of the Son and of the Holy Spirit', although in the Acts of the Apostles baptism seems to have been simply 'in the name of Jesus'. This surely reflects the developing experience of the Christians: they had been created by the Father and rescued by the Son but also empowered and taught by the Spirit or Energy ('of the Father' or 'of Christ' in Paul's letters). Paul reminded the Christians in Rome (in chapter 8) that 'God's Spirit dwells in you', affirms that 'we are God's children' and 'comes to the aid of our weakness', praying in us when 'we do not even know how we ought to pray'. But nowhere in the New Testament is it said that we can know how the Father, the Son and the Spirit are eternally related to each other.

What we can believe if we believe the New Testament's good news is that the one God has acted towards us in three ways, for to us the Creator is now somewhat like the father to whom we owe our conception; Jesus is now somewhat like the son who represents his father; the Spirit is somewhat like our best friend. And these are not trivial beliefs. Our entire attitude to the universe around us is changed if we think that it is the work of the God whose purpose is loving. Our lives are transformed if we think that Jesus is the human face of God's love. Our emotions and thoughts are very different if we think that we can be, and have been, electrified by the energy of this loving God. And out of these experiences we can draw a reasonable belief that now and eternally the Father loves Jesus, and Jesus loves the Father, with the energy of love that is the Spirit. Beyond this we mortals cannot talk or think meaningfully – and beyond this we have no need to go. Indeed, most Christians probably have no wish to go. What they have actually experience would make them more or less satisfied with the ancient and simple image of the 'triune' God as being like a human being who works with two hands. They have a healthy impatience with speculations which venture far beyond faith based on experience, and although some theologians have been, and are, more foolishly confident, a very brief inspection of the history of the doctrine of the Trinity will show that the deepest theologians have avoided treating the 'persons' in the divine unity as three people.

The Latin *persona* translated the Greek *hypostasis*, and neither word was intended to suggest that Christians believe in three divine individuals – in other words, in three gods. The great Augustine, writing in Latin, compared the Trinity with three faculties of one person (memory, understanding and will, or elsewhere intellect, knowledge and love). The Fathers of the Church, writing in Greek, stressed that the Father is the *arché* (origin) of the other Two and that there is no separation between the activities of the Three although they can be distinguished in human thought about human experience. *Hypostasis* never meant 'person' in the modern sense: a more accurate (although less attractive) translation would be 'instance of an essence', since *hypostasis* answered the question 'which is it?' while *ousia* (Being) answered the question 'what is it?'

Thus the best theologians acknowledged both the mystery and the unity of God. They did not obscure the fact that the Lord they worshipped had himself declared total belief in, and total love for, the One God to be the first of all the commandments; as a devout Jew he must have recited this *Shema* every morning and every evening. But theology could also be overconfident in its dogmas about the two 'natures' and 'wills' of the incarnate Son and it is clear that this soaring arrogance resulted both in divisions between Christians who claimed to be orthodox and in a loss of confidence when the armies of Islam swept out of the desert. The Arabs were great soldiers but the most effective of their weapons was their conviction that their Prophet had been given the one true revelation of the one true God and of the one right way of living in submission to that God. To this day all Muslims share that faith, knowing that no theme is more emphatic in the teaching of the Quran itself. If there is to be any fruitful dialogue between the world's two largest religions, the question whether Christians really do believe in One God must be answered without any equivocation. In the dialogue with Judaism, which has now begun after an immensely tragic delay, the same question is vital. Hindus, whose belief in One God has been deepened by the challenge of the Christian mission in India, also ask questions if Christians now speak of a 'dance' of the Three. And the right answer seems to be that if anyone now believes that Jesus was, and is, a man in and through whom the One God was, and is, uniquely active and best revealed, there is the heart of Christian belief because there is agreement with the New Testament's central message.

It will be a further tragedy if Christian faith in the 'triune' God is presented in such a way that it seems to be polytheism with multiple gods and helps to make Christianity appear totally unbelievable in confrontation with modern atheism. The tragedy would be unnecessary. A good recent discussion is *Jesus the Symbol of God* by a Jesuit scholar, Roger Haight (1999); and Henry Chadwick's *The Church in Ancient Society* (2002), the masterwork of a great scholar, recounted the theological debate in Christianity's first 600 years.

*   *   *

At first sight there is no connection between this chapter and the discussion about glimpses of God in the age of science. But there is a strong link. It is helpful that Gerd Theissen has explored *Biblical Faith* in connection with evolution (1994) and is the co-author with Annette Merz of a guide to the scholarly literature about *The Historical Jesus* (1998).

Modern knowledge of evolution raises a moral question because here is a process which consistently favours the strong against the weak, and the moral sense of humans can find this repulsive. Many other creatures protect, feed and train their young and support the group to which they belong, and in such instincts may be found the evolutionary preliminaries to the human sense of right and wrong, but the strength of the human conscience seems to be unique in nature and one of the commands of the conscience is that the weak should not be crushed. In contrast, nature appears to be utterly ruthless in its preference for the strong in any conflict or competition and in its use of the weaker as food for the stronger. If we pause to think calmly, we may see that living beings (ourselves among them) can continue to live only if they absorb into their systems food provided by simpler chemical structures: much as plants feed on inorganic materials, so some animals feed on plants and some on other animals. We may see that, and we may accept it as inevitable if plants and animals are to exist, but when we are not eating meat (but perhaps watching one animal kill another on TV) we may not like what we see.

In the Book of Job the Creator answers this human protest by a speech which takes pride in the strongest features of nature and in the strongest living creatures, reckoned to be the eagle, the whale and the crocodile. His point is not explained theoretically but it seems to be a justification of strength as the Creator's finest achievement, urging Job to stand up 'like a man'. Yet in the Hebrew Bible taken as a whole, the Lord of history is on the side of the weak, beginning with the rescue of the *Hapiru*, disorganized outcasts on the margins of society, and in the Christian Bible the Father's message is good news not for the strong but for the poor, the prisoners, the blind and society's broken victims (Luke 4.16–21). The final blessing of God is on those who bring food to the hungry, drink to the thirsty, a welcome to strangers and dignity to the naked (Matthew 25.31–46). And Christ who is 'in the form of God' is himself weak, 'even to the point of death, death on a cross!' (Philippians 2.6, 8). So the supreme revelation is in the cross, not the crocodile, for the Creator of all strength utters the most significant of all words in an infant, a carpenter, an outlaw and a nailed-down victim, before the strangest of all victories is won. The Church that could be more Christian would be a Church preaching 'Christ crucified' as the self-disclosure of God – and living under the cross, alongside the weak, including those who feel Godforsaken.

CHAPTER 4

Government by God

THE TWO HALVES of what I learned by living in the centre of London were joined by a street, Whitehall.

It was in the church overlooking Trafalgar Square that I saw Christian welcome and help to the lonely, the unhappy and the desperate, and so 'saw' Jesus alive and at work – but over the years I have also learned by watching life in the square itself. When the English weather permits, or when Christmas or the New Year makes people forget it, Trafalgar Square is probably the happiest outdoor place in London. People of all ages gravitate here in good humour, as equals from all over society and as tourists from all over the world. This space at the heart of a city even provides some contacts with nature: pigeons are fed, fountains are enjoyed. By a very long tradition it is also a natural place for demonstrations calling for justice and peace in a response to the wrongs of the world.

As a traveller catches the first close sight of a new country by looking down on an airport (but an airport is only one place in the country), I have seen in this square something of the kingdom of God announced by Jesus: unregimented people enjoying themselves together harmlessly or voicing anger against injustice and violence. The scene is informally relaxed or vigorously democratic, but whether or not people would connect it with religion it can be viewed by a Christian as a little part of the fulfilment of the visionary hopes of the prophet from Nazareth. It presents an alternative to the centuries commemorated in the square's monuments to men victorious in war – and an alternative to much inhumanity in the centuries of religion.

But I have also lived at the other end of Whitehall. There I was made to think about this 'kingdom' glimpsed in the happiness or the protests of Trafalgar Square. Does the proclamation by Jesus about government by God mean, in effect, success and power for the Church? Or does it refer chiefly to heaven? These were interpretations of the idea prominent in the Middle Ages, when the Church was triumphant and Europe was Christendom. But at the other end of Whitehall I was made to see that these were misconceptions, and I was not entirely surprised by what I learned. Anyone reading the gospels with care can see that Jesus expected his followers to be few and unpopular but did not teach that they should therefore despair about life before death. And anyone can also see that Jesus did not rely on his disciples for the arrival of the kingdom of God.

In 1970 I began eight years as a canon of Westminster Abbey and for most of that time I was also the Speaker's Chaplain in the House of Commons. This position made a considerable contrast to my earlier experience of the Church being treated as marginal. On the high altar of the Abbey are inscribed words from the Revelation of John (11.15): 'The kingdoms of the world are become the kingdom of our Lord and of his Christ.' In the dramatic enactment of an alliance between throne and altar, a monarch is consecrated in front of this altar, anointed with holy oil, given a globe-like orb topped by a cross, and crowned with a glittering exhibition of sovereignty under the same sign of royal allegiance to Christ. And every day the business of the House of Commons begins with a psalm (67) and with a prayer acknowledging the sovereignty of God over princes and peoples, and therefore petitioning that the humble representatives of the mere 'commons' should be inspired to set aside 'all private interests and partial affections'.

A visitor arriving in Westminster after an interplanetary flight might therefore gain a first impression that Britain is a theocracy, not entirely unlike Iran, for example – a society controlled by a political power which is itself obedient to the teachings of a religion as declared by that religion's official representatives. That impression would not be entirely foolish. The Palace of Westminster where Parliament meets was reconstructed in the Victorian age with a medieval look, and the society to which its architecture harks back was indeed close to being a theocracy. From the fourth Christian century the church called Catholic or Orthodox decided the religion and morality of the whole Roman or Byzantine Empire, at least in theory, and although power was mainly in the emperor's hands the emperor knew that to maintain his power he needed the church as well as the army. Much of this system survived in the era of nationalism and Protestantism, with Church and State together controlling belief and behaviour.

But of course a closer inspection of real life in modern Westminster, or anywhere else in the modern world, would soon show that the old system has broken down, for a whole host of reasons. What has replaced it may be called democracy although obviously much remains to be done in order to make a modern state more completely democratic – and after the end of the *ancien régime* with its powerful alliance of throne and altar has come a general lack of interest in what the representatives of religion may say about affairs of state. What a modern politician needs is the blessing of the people.

Although the Speakers under whom I served, Selwyn Lloyd and George Thomas, were both Methodists and the latter was a well-known preacher, and although I knew that many MPs were also Christians, and although I was never treated by anyone with anything but courtesy, few MPs attended the prayers which I recited (and which had not been changed since the reign of Charles II, apart from the names of the Royal Family). It is a convention, in my view healthy, that MPs' religious convictions should not be mentioned in the course of a debate about politics and for my part I learned not to offer advice on the detailed questions of the day when wearing a clerical collar and surrounded by politicians – perhaps in my most successful imitation of Christ who asked a man with a financial grievance: 'Who set me over you to judge or arbitrate?' (Luke 12.14).

I was also the rector of St Margaret's church, a position which illustrated for me how depressing are the difficulties faced by many people who find themselves responsible for churches built to serve the needs of another age and now demanding much time and money for their maintenance. It can be very hard to discern the connection between those crumbling monuments and the urgent mission of our own time. We did, however, manage to put this historic church on a new basis: that needed a special Act of Parliament, and as other solutions are found for other problems I can only admire other groups which are taking action. A few churches need to be demolished or sold and others can be kept open for prayers and visits rather than for regular services (with temptations to thieves removed) – but some can earn their keep by being used not only for worship but also for 'community' purposes, and many examples already exist in the revival of this usage which was common in the Middle Ages.

Since the time when the seventeenth-century Puritans had wanted to hear their favourite preachers at length, St Margaret's had enjoyed the proud status of being the parish church of the House of Commons. In the past it had also been the busy church of a large parish, mostly rural for many centuries but for a time heavily populated by a mixture of the poor and the grand. But when I arrived the remnant left of the old parish had few residents and it did not mean much that in Anglican theory I was responsible for the spiritual welfare of Downing Street and a few other roads. The regular congregation was even smaller, and depressingly they gathered in a building which was dirty and crumbling because of the filth which had for long polluted London's air. An appeal for funds seemed to be impossible because the neighbouring Abbey was about to ask for many millions, also needed for urgent repairs, and a rescue by taxpayers was even further out of the question.

Fortunately we were able to find a way to save this historic church by making it more useful under present conditions – a way which seems obvious now but did not look like that to everyone at the time. It was transferred to the care and control of its neighbour, Westminster Abbey. As a result it can be used not only for a continuing congregation's regular worship but also for many special events, held there when the Abbey is not conveniently available, and this wider usefulness has been important for the success of appeals for the large sums needed for its fabric, its organ and its general appearance. It can stand in its admittedly extraordinary position as something of a symbol of many possibilities in renewal, now that the Church has been deprived of what the world regards as triumph.

*   *   *

In Westminster I was also made well aware that although churchgoing is no longer popular, churches and their clergy are still used for funerals and memorial services. I had to ask: does this suggest that the Church ought to concentrate on eternity and on preparation for it? The Abbey had been founded some 900 years ago because an Anglo-Saxon king wanted a monastery next to his palace, and it had received many endowments in the Middle Ages because the Catholic Church had claimed power over eternity: people excommunicated by it should not expect to be forgiven by God, and people who were average and therefore sinners should expect to spend an unpleasant time in purgatory, a time which could, however, be shortened by the Church's prayers. Medieval kings and queens had been buried in this monastery where they had been crowned, ending with Henry VII, regarded in his day as a miser but the builder of a sumptuous and well-endowed chapel which was to be the scene of prayers for his soul to the end of time.

Since the Middle Ages Westminster Abbey and St Margaret's have continued to commemorate the dead, although without any suggestion that the Church is in control of them. Distinguished people have been buried in church or churchyard, or honoured by monuments large or modest. Many memorial services have gathered large congregations to hear carefully prepared addresses assessing the dead charitably. The Abbey has been called a temple of silence and reconciliation since many controversies, once fierce, have been buried within its embracing walls along with many other symbols of the history of England (Darwin is buried there, near Newton). At all these ceremonies of farewell eternity has also been remembered, as the conclusion to all human busyness including politics. And I could not doubt that when providing these opportunities to think about the meanings of lives, and of life itself, the Church was being useful – as its representatives are still useful, and appreciated, in most of the funerals throughout Britain. But . . .

The use of the term 'kingdom of Heaven' in Matthew's gospel is not a reference to life after death: it refers to life under God in a kingdom to come on earth, as is made clear every time that the Lord's Prayer is recited. The parables of Jesus picture the kingdom growing on earth like corn amid weeds or grapes on a vine, and even being in the soil like seeds or buried treasure. The teaching of Jesus excites people to be alert for the arrival and full growth of this kingdom on earth, to enter it, to receive it and to enjoy it. Almost certainly a passage in Luke's gospel (17.20, 21) means that the kingdom is already beginning in 'the midst of you', within the grasp of those who stand around Jesus asking when it will come. It would be against the whole teaching of this gospel to think that the Greek word *entos* in this report of the reply by Jesus is intended to mean that the kingdom is 'within' the individual as a spiritual and moral condition, producing a religion which is essentially private and other-worldly.

Of course there are spiritual and moral conditions for entry into the kingdom of which Jesus spoke: his parables make that clear, too. Indeed, his great interpreters Paul and John, aware that talk about a new kingdom could very easily be mistaken for talk about rebellion against Rome, made very little use of the word now translated as 'kingdom'. To Paul the kingdom is 'justice, peace and joy, inspired by the Holy Spirit' (Romans 14.17) and a list can be made of wrong-doers who cannot 'inherit' it. The fourth gospel mentions the kingdom in one passage only, when Nicodemus is told that no one can enter it without being born 'again' or 'from above' (3.3–15). But what lies behind the use of 'kingdom' in the other gospels (about 100 times) is shown when Jesus is executed. Pilate does not punish him for talking in general terms about justice, peace and joy and a spiritual rebirth, or for being a healer and a critic of priests and rabbis. To Roman eyes Jesus is dangerous because he can be called 'King of the Jews' – and because he cannot deny that the kingdom which he has proclaimed must end in the government of the world by God.

It is clear that Jesus hoped that this transformation of the world would come quickly. The early Christians were sure about this – and shared the hope. Matthew's gospel, for example, begins with the proclamation that 'the kingdom of Heaven is open to you' or 'has come near' (4.17). When the twelve disciples are sent out on their first mission they are told that they 'will not have gone through all the towns of Israel before the Son of Man will have come' (10.23). When Jesus has seen that he must die before this triumphant 'coming' (16.21), he still hopes that 'this generation will not pass away' (24.34) before 'all the peoples of the world' see 'the Son of Man coming in the clouds of heaven with power and great glory' to 'gather his elect from the four winds' (24.30, 31). The image is of a journey from heaven to earth but the reference is to the vision in the Book of Daniel (7.13, 14): 'one like a son of man' goes to God 'with the clouds of heaven' and is given 'sovereignty and glory and kingly power' over 'all peoples and nations'. There the vision is interpreted as meaning that the 'holy ones of the most high' will 'possess the kingdom for ever' because they have survived all the cruelty of the empires. It is a promise to Jewish saints and martyrs that they will be vindicated. In Matthew's gospel (as elsewhere) Jesus calls himself the 'Son of Man', an expression which can mean no more than 'a man' but which is here used very solemnly. It indicates that he expects vindication by God before the whole of living humanity. A crucial moment comes when the high priest is told that 'from now on you will see the Son of Man seated at the right hand of the Almighty and coming on the clouds of heaven' (26.64) – a claim which leads directly to the cross.

All that seems reasonably clear in Matthew's gospel – yet this gospel also shows that the early Christians considered it quite possible that the full vindication of their Lord would not be quick: here are strong warnings against false hopes and an expectation that 'this good news of the kingdom will be proclaimed throughout the earth' before 'the end will come' (24.14).

The same warnings are prominent in Mark's gospel, which Matthew has used: there will be wars, persecutions and false Messiahs, presumably taking a considerable time. Only 'the one who endures to the end will be saved' and 'about that hour no one knows, not even the angels in heaven, not even the Son; no one but the Father' (13.13, 32). Mark seems to have used here an even earlier document, for the reader is asked not to get too excited about the attempt by the mad emperor Caligula in AD 40 to have his statue installed in the Jerusalem temple (13.14). Evidently the admission of ignorance about 'that hour' was not put into the mouth of Jesus after a prolonged disappointment: it comes from a tradition earlier than Paul's letters.

Paul was probably typical of the first generation of Christians when he urged the Philippians to rejoice because the 'day of Jesus Christ' was 'near' – yet for himself, he accepted the nearness of union with Christ through death and considered it 'far better' than being alive to see that day arriving on earth (1.6, 20–25; 4.5). When a later document, 2 Peter, was written Christians were asking 'What has happened to his promised coming?' but they could be reminded of two points already firmly in their tradition: whatever picture may be formed about the end of history, their Lord would 'come' as he had himself expected, as a surprise like a burglar in the night – and whatever may be human impatience, 'in the Lord's sight one day is like a thousand years and a thousand years like one day' (3.4, 8). To this writer neither the circumstances nor the time of the Lord's 'coming' could be known in advance.

It seems that in history as in nature God is active in ways beyond human understanding, and in particular beyond our capacity to predict the future – but that glimpses of God's work are possible when we see the results of the mysterious activity, taken as a whole.

And in Westminster, as I believe, I saw some of the results. While life in the Christian Church, however humble, is meant to be a model showing what life can be, and life in this world is meant to be a preparation for an eternal share in the divine life, there are signs that the government of this world by God has made some progress outside the Church but inside life before death. That ought to be said more loudly and celebrated more gratefully. What was in front of my eyes in Westminster was of course only a small part of the work of God in every period and every place, and in every individual's life – the work of strengthening everything that makes for good, however feeble that piece of humanity may be, and the work of fighting and destroying what is evil, however powerful evil may be in systems or in hearts. Our vision of the 'coming' kingdom of God ought to be no narrower than that. But Westminster made me see a part of God's work which is not insignificant, being an example of the inspiration and use of a human government.

*   *   *

Martin Luther said that God has two hands: with one he rules the Church through the Word and Sacraments, with the other he rules the world through the 'orders of creation' which include marriage to control sexuality and the state to control anarchy. This doctrine proved to be as dangerous as the medieval Church's claim to be the supreme governor of society, for it was to be corrupted into much Lutheran support for princes, for militarists and for Hitler (a record matched in other churches). But essentially it was in keeping with the New Testament. Jesus accepted the authority of Pilate to inflict capital punishment and Paul wrote about the emperor Nero, under whom he was to be martyred, as possessing an authority derived from God (Romans 13.1). So when serving in Westminster I had to ask what it meant realistically to repeat the biblical and traditional doctrine that the state is an institution blessed and used by God in the course of the establishment of his own rule on earth as in heaven.

The Speaker's Chaplain is given a worm's-eye view of the House of Commons, so that I was able to watch some of the business of government and debate in a modern parliamentary democracy at fairly close quarters. I did so during years when no one could think that any government's task was easy, or that criticism of the government must be mild. The post-war consensus around a planned economy and a welfare state was over: the Conservatives were making the transition from Heath to Thatcher and the Labour Party was making its move from government under Wilson to unelectability too far on the Left. In economics Britain could then be described as the sick man of Europe, with inflation as the most obvious symptom.

This was a depressing atmosphere but in it I learned two truths. One is that the New Testament's vision of the kingdom of God includes what in the Old Testament is called *shalom*, social justice with peaceful prosperity for all, and therefore the Church must proclaim that vision as a part of its unchanging and unstoppable message. Any group which by selfishness or incompetence resists *shalom* is guilty of some kind of sin. The other is that the problems in achieving *shalom* are likely to be complex and controversial, making most political decisions a fallible choice between shades of grey, so that although individuals who belong to churches or speak for them are perfectly entitled – indeed, obliged – to develop and offer practical suggestions where possible, it is rarely the function of the Church as such to take sides in disputes about particular proposals. What seems to be the will of God is that a modern democratic state, with a government given power for a term but answerable to an electorate, to free media, to independent law courts and (not least) to political opponents, should be the sphere in which the vision is translated into laws and actions which are good enough for the time being.

If that is the case, then it is sad and wrong that so many citizens of a democracy should neglect to vote in elections – and equally sad and wrong that so many commentators, incuding preachers, should neglect to affirm some respect for those involved in the political process. Although it can easily be thought in connection with politics that being 'prophetic' means denouncing politicians, Westminster taught me that celebration can be a part of the prophecy – and the Bible also teaches this. Criticism is necessary but not enough. If the Creator is the Father of all, what is the 'common good' but the flourishing of all the children of God? And in Christian eyes what is the work done by the state for the common good, if it is not work for the kingdom of God? And if in the past kings could be said to rule 'by divine right', authorized by God, cannot MPs be prayed for with hope?

I learned to marvel at the massive equipment which a modern democratic state has for this work. In Britain in recent years it has become the convention that public expenditure should be at a level not far from 40 per cent of the nation's total income – and we all know that what finances that budget does not grow on trees. Although in the centuries when the Church was politically powerful such taxation would have been inconceivable, now that the convention is established it seems appropriate for the Church to defend it, never lamenting the loss of its past control over healing, education and other works of charity. What is now being done, on a scale which would astonish us if we did not take it for granted, is justice – which is God's will and demand.

I learned to admire the work of those who direct the operation of the giant machine which is the modern state – and the work of those who are the human bits in this machine. Decision-makers in national or local government are bombarded with criticism, and the civil servants who advise them or execute their orders are despised as 'red tape' – but without them, citizens would be in a very different state. And I learned that the largely hidden service given by MPs and local councillors to their constituents (of all parties) is not unlike the pastoral work of the clergy – often not rewarded by the affection given to the clergy but often more effective in meeting practical needs.

I also learned that reactions in religious groups to new legislation can be misjudged. It is not the duty of a democratic state to incorporate in its laws the moral positions accepted only by a minority. Public opinion may be mistaken about facts (it has been in its belief that capital punishment deters murderers, and it still is in its belief that imprisonment without education changes criminals), but on matters of opinion it is wrong for legislation to be either far ahead or far behind the majority in the electorate. In the 1970s it was therefore right to defend legislation of the 1960s which reflected the changes in public attitudes to divorce and abortion, to censorship and to homosexual practices between consenting adults. It is not the proper role of any church to lay down the law in defiance of public opinion.

Thus Westminster taught me much about the religious significance of national governments, and I am sure that much the same is true of local government, but it also gave me other glimpses of the coming of the kingdom of God.

* * *

For seven years I was the chairman of a great charity, Christian Aid, supporting two directors whose abilities were outstanding, Alan Booth and Kenneth Slack (both Free Church ministers). Here, too, it was a time of tensions. Some of the staff and voluntary workers wanted the emphasis to be on charity, through projects which could be identified as gifts from the British churches to the world's poorest people. For others, charity was less important than justice and their main interest was in campaigning to end the situation in which governments, including our own, failed to reach the UN target for official aid of 0.7 per cent of a nation's income – and in which the great transnational companies, often with more resources than some governments, could stand above any law (it might be, on the basis of bribes to government ministers in the underdeveloped countries). The tensions between the 'charity' and 'justice' enthusiasts could be acute but we did all that we could to keep the two groups within the one movement by constantly stressing that Christian Aid was no more – and no less – than an instrument of the churches. Our grants were sent to the Christians on the spot as contributions to a multitude of relief or development projects often too small to interest governments and to tempt corruption – and therefore uniquely valuable as prophetic signs that the kingdom of God must include the worldwide end of dehumanizing poverty. This aim was accepted both by our partners overseas and, in our own country, by an army of collectors who every year since 1957 in Christian Aid Week went from door to door asking their neighbours for donations and offering in return a willingness to discuss any objection that aid would be wasted. I remain convinced that this appeal for charity at people's front doors was the best possible campaign for justice, and I would guess that it had something to do with the success – of course not complete – of the later campaign to celebrate the new millennium by reducing the burden of debt on the world's poorest countries.

In many emergencies around the world the response of charity through the aid agencies has been essential. Like Oxfam (founded by Christians in Oxford), Christian Aid (led by Janet Lacey, an unorthodox saint) was a response to the ruin of continental Europe left behind by the Second World War. The European churches were themselves now very poor and destitute millions had no homes, so that originally this aid from British churchgoers was called the 'Inter-church Aid and Refugee Service'. The Christian imperative to imitate the good Samaritan was simple and required simple actions,

and that simplicity has inspired a generosity which has grown from
year to year as disasters have not ceased. Of course it is all to the
good that non-churchgoers have also responded massively, often in
response to the overwhelming impact of TV, and it is another sign of
the coming of the kingdom of God amid tragedies that the awareness of the roles of the UN and of national governments has also
grown. They have immensely larger resources in money and com-
munications for the immediate relief of millions who are desperate.
In the longer term they alone can decide how national economies
and international trade can develop to the benefit of the many, not
the privileged. However, they can do little or nothing without determined and consistent support or pressure from the peoples of the
world. That can be inspired from many sources, and driven by many
motives, but it seems reasonable to believe that no motive can be
more powerful than the conviction that the God who is the Creator
and Father of all urgently demands justice for all. This is the most
important reason why an explicitly Christian charity has a function
which is basically – of course not entirely – different from the tasks
of non-religious charities or governments, for a Christian charity can
speak openly of the God who is determined to govern the world
without being a dictator over the disastrous evil and folly of
humans. And for a Christian charity, each act of charity is a prophetic sign that this government is taking power, and a parable about
what justice therefore means.

*   *   *

During my earlier time in London I had already been involved in a
cause no less important than the relief of poverty: thinking in
response to the danger that the all-out use of nuclear weapons would
create many new Hiroshimas and Nagasakis. This involvement had
started when some of us were shocked to find a senior bishop
accepting the possibility of an exchange of total destruction with the
'better dead than Red' argument. This was a time when it was very
seriously feared that Britain would be a victim in the actual use of
'strategic' missiles and when detailed plans were made for retaliation
on the same scale of horror. The Defence White Paper of 1955 had
also contemplated the possibility of escalation to nuclear war at the
apocalyptic level by the use of 'tactical' nuclear weapons to repel an
attack by an army on the ground, even if the other side had not used
such weapons first. That was a policy called by a wit 'surrender or

suicide', but it had the advantage that a large army of conscripts would not be needed. In this connection I had written a pamphlet entitled *Withdrawing from the Brink* in 1963.

At a time when the Red Army still dominated Eastern Europe and threatened the West, it was a plea to stand back from a rush to a nuclear response. Nineteen years later a group appointed by the Church of England had a much larger impact with a report entitled *The Church and the Bomb*. This advocated Britain's unilateral nuclear disarmament but not its withdrawal from nuclear-armed NATO and there was a tense debate about it in the General Synod, reaching the public as a broadcast and ending in the rejection of a policy which would have disturbed the 'balance of terror' which was widely believed to prevent a Third World War.

Our anxious agitations did something to keep morality alive in such a time but otherwise did not achieve much. Uranium-tipped shells have been used and in our new century Polaris submarines capable of wiping out a city prowl in the ocean. In 2002 nuclear disarmament seems so impossible that India and Pakistan feel that they must afford membership of this club and a president of the USA has propounded the dream that 100 per cent of incoming missiles could be destroyed in mid-air as an answer to what could arrive from a 'rogue state'. And what ended the mad arms race of the Cold War was not moral outrage: it was the collapse of the Soviet economy, which could not afford the competition. So it is easy to draw the dismaying conclusion that these and other satanic weapons are here to stay. But one must not complain when the facts of life support arguments based on ethics – and two useful institutions emerged out of a conference which some of us arranged in Brighton back in the 1960s: the International Institute of Strategic Studies, working for a much more sophisticated awareness of the realities, and the much smaller Council on Christian Approaches to Defence and Disarmament. And now?

I write after 11 September 2001, when suicidal mass-murderers began to change many things. It seems possible that those humans who want to continue to live on this planet may be entering a new period combining morality and realism about war – and that the worldwide Church could be in a position to lead them.

Originally Christianity was pacifist but gradually Christians were allowed by the Church to serve in the army (preferably in non-combatant roles) and it was not long before everyone in the Roman

Empire's army had to be a Christian (apart from hired mercenaries).That period was followed by much support for the armed forces of the divided nations by the divided churches. Nowadays, however, Christians are among those who have to make decisions about war and peace, as leaders or voters, and increasingly consciences are troubled. Although most of us know in our hearts that war can never be more than the lesser of two evils, most of us know also that a war can be a very tragic necessity when it stands a real chance of stopping aggression or terrorism and aims at military targets only (not deliberately killing civilians). This seems to be an updated version of the doctrines about a 'just war' worked out long ago by St Augustine and St Thomas Aquinas. But it is also widely agreed that the facts of modern war demand a new vision – as do the facts about the modern spread of nuclear or 'conventional' weapons in the hands of states or individuals. Being the world's only remaining superpower with a capacity to use devastating force in retaliation, and having a centuries-old assumption that oceans separate the 'new world' from the troubles of the old, cannot provide security after what struck the World Trade Center on that September morning. And even that solitary superpower cannot safely make a unilateral decision as to when to shoot as the world's policeman. So if pacifism still seems escapist, the 'just war' tradition now seems outdated. Has the time come for a worldwide campaign for a disarmament which must include almost all arms and absolutely all nations?

In this terrible light it has become clear, for 'realistic' as well as moral reasons, that no war can be called 'just' unless it is accepted as necessary by all the nations not clearly prejudiced in favour of the aggressor. We may also be beginning to agree that no nation on Earth is entitled to possess its own weapons of mass destruction – or to be lax about the private possession of guns, or to export arms to other nations except at the low level needed to maintain their internal security without supporting a regime's ability to deny the human rights of its own people. Any nation claiming exemption from such disarmament should unite all other nations in effective sanctions against it. Even the USA should not be exempt – and that superpower's flourishing churches need to say so courageously.

Hitherto any such vision of a disarmed world has seemed to be a completely utopian dream: the nations which ought to have been most aware that power brings responsibility have developed, stockpiled and sold arms, even pleading that such 'defence' and 'exports' are necessary in order to provide jobs for their own citizens, while in nations which ought to have concentrated on a war against poverty scarce resources have been poured into the purchase of arms and civil wars have been fought fanatically in the belief that it is noble to ruin one's own country. But for humanity's sake and therefore for God's sake, an alternative to this madness must be found soon. And it seems that there is no alternative except what may be called (however provocatively) the government of the world by the United Nations when that is needed in order to stop what has become intolerable. Even in times of peace a permanent and effective UN agency for intelligence and inspection is essential in order to fight the development and spread of arms in preparation for international or civil war, or for terrorism. With such an agency in place, the world would still run risks – but it runs many more now.

The problems are obvious, but already there have been signs to arouse hope. Already the dangers involved in even possessing weapons of mass destruction are appreciated so widely that it does not seem totally unrealistic to hope for international action. Already terrorism is condemned so widely that within three months of 11 September 2001 victories had been won – and in recent history the Balkans had been pacified by an international coalition. Winning a war can be easier than keeping a peace, but when an international force can stand between the hatreds in Cyprus (for example) it does not seem merely sentimental to hope that by the pressure of the international community justice and peace can be brought even to Jerusalem and the Holy Land.

*   *   *

When I left Westminster for more normal duties I was of course far less involved in such questions, but the new Archbishop of Canterbury, Robert Runcie, encouraged me to work with a Tory MP, Michael Alison, on a book of essays which resulted from a substantial series of meetings between some of Margaret Thatcher's closest associates and some of her critics, and with others who were more detached from the controversies of the day. It was called *Christianity and Conservatism* (1990).

Our discussion ranged over a minefield of political and economic problems, but we agreed that as Christians we needed two guides all the time. We could not rely only on secular sources of knowledge and wisdom, because they did not include the haunting and commanding vision of the kingdom of God – but also, we could not rely solely on the Bible, for that was written in times remote from our current affairs. And that agreement about method in a Christian approach was not our only agreement. I now quote from just four paragraphs which I added to our book, because I want to argue that the agreement which we reached was not a bad example of the fact that when Christians take trouble they can talk sense about public affairs, although not necessarily about day-to-day problems.

It has been discovered in modern times that the most effective way to create wealth, ultimately for the benefit of all, is to allow individuals and enterprises to compete in a free market, retaining most of their profits to add to their private property. The ownership of the means of production, distribution and exchange by the state or by a firm's employees is less likely to be progressive in the creation of wealth. A Bible-based Christianity (including both Testaments) teaches that the Creator blesses wealth creation provided that it does not become an obsession and is properly used. Therefore in modern times Christians may rightly regard the free market as something given by God, like the state and the family.

But the market has its limits. Unless they are guided and modified by the whole community acting partly through the state, market forces do not do enough for job creation, for the dignity of the worker, for health, education and social security, for the arts or for other causes which Christians value. It is impossible to quantify success or efficiency in such causes if one relies solely on the criteria of the market.

The chief purpose of wealth creation through the market (thus limited) is to make easier, and to encourage, a richly human life. This must involve the strengthening of family life as the greatest earthly source of human happiness, the strengthening of many other communities on a human scale, and the strengthening of the individual's sense of being responsible and accountable for making the most of the fragile gift of life. The Christian will add very emphatically that every person is responsible and accountable to God, who as holy love both demands and enables an ultimate perfection.

A greater unity and a higher prosperity seem to be attainable in Europe including Britain during the 1990s. It appears to be possible to create a society better as well as richer than any in the past. The necessary work will provide profoundly exciting and challenging opportunities for Christians – chiefly the laity – to make theoretical or practical contributions. These contributions may be made within what is somewhat oddly called the Conservative tradition. They may also be made in other ways.

One can, I believe, add a few more truths without descending into party politics. New Labour won a landslide victory in the election of 1997 because it had accepted an idea previously regarded as the monopoly of modern Conservatism – the idea that wealth is now created mainly by private businesses competing in a free market. This was a great and painful change and the churches could have offered sympathy during the pangs of Labour's rebirth, for in church-related thought about the problems of society the solution had for many years seemed to be some kind of Christian Socialism. But since socialism, defined by its idealistic pioneers as meaning very extensive public ownership, has turned out to mean in practice deci-sion-making by politicians with limited shrewdness, bureaucrats with limited skill or workers' representatives with limited foresight, socialism cannot deliver the goods wanted by consumers. Like Britain, the Soviet Union and China learned that.

But in Britain the Conservatives unintentionally made way for New Labour, for what came across to the public from them was an ideology as unappealing as socialism. Rightly they admired enter-prising wealth-creation but they gave the impression of being apologetic about maintaining expenditure on the public services while the electorate knew that private enterprise could never be expected to finance by itself these services which seemed both essen-tial and in need of larger resources. The excited talk on the Right was of rolling back the state, taking an axe to taxes, and setting the people free – but the bulk of the public never warmed to proposals that the state should become so restricted, and taxes so low, that the average citizen would be left free to suffer.

The Conservatives were on much stronger ground when they defended the family, the local community and personal responsibil-ity ('back to basics'), but they could not mount an effective defence because they were not sensitive enough to see fully how things had changed. In the Victorian age the churches had been the most influential of the institutions which sustained the traditional values: the family was made sacred by solemn rites in church, the local community knew where and what a church was, the children could go to Sunday School. But since then many forces have buffeted that traditional family, shattered or reshaped communities, and provided many new reasons or excuses for behaviour with little or no sense of responsibility to others, while the attempts of the churches to reaffirm the old values have usually been made on the basis of beliefs which the bulk of the public now regards as incredible. Whereas in the old days the Conservative Party agreed (at least in theory) that the values taught by the churches were the values which ought to be defended, by the end of the twentieth century its links with the churches had largely lost intellectual and moral strength – and no new vision of a good society which might arise out of the transforming changes had reached the leadership, let alone the electorate.

In 2002 it seems uncertain whether the Conservatives will ever copy Labour by becoming electable while in the political wilderness. Although probably churchgoers have tended to vote for this party rather than for any other (unlike church leaders), this support may well belong to tradition rather than to the future. But it is clear that, whether or not they are in their own wilderness, Britain's churches have a duty to set an example to all politicians by rethinking what now deserves to be conserved.

*   *   *

One of the transforming changes since the 1950s is that, however reluctantly, the British electorate has ceased to be surprised by a phrase such as 'Europe including Britain'. A Conservative government 'took Britain into Europe' (as another phrase went) but after the removal of Edward Heath the nostalgia for the isolation of an island grew, after the removal of Margaret Thatcher it split the party, and after the defeat of John Major it prevailed. In the churches, too, Euroscepticism or Euroindifference has been strong but Britain's churches have on the whole resisted the temptation to gain a cheap popularity by selling their souls to nationalism, and this seems to be the result of being aware that neither religious nor social salvation can be made in Britain alone. To walk into a church is – or according to the church's teaching ought to be – walking into the world. As the churches themselves walk into the future amid many British voices which declare them irrelevant, they are entitled to reflect that after the criticism which came from them against some (not all) aspects of Conservatism in power, voting in elections proved them to be right in the terms of democratic politics. This memory of a great vindication should encourage them to speak up about what the rebirth of Europe means positively.

My *Christians in a New Europe*, also published in 1990, was the first book of its kind to appear in any language and much of it was an account of the development of the European Union (as it was to become in 1992). An uplifting story began with the surge of determination to prevent any future war and with the foundation of the European Community in 1957, but I had to record that Britain had felt so superior to continental dreams that its entry was not achieved before 1973, and ten years later 'renegotiation' (which would have meant exit) was demanded in the Labour Party's election manifesto. Then the story got bogged down in a swamp of difficulties as 'community' or 'union' or 'federation' had to be redefined by nations each with its own agenda and by politicians who were all too human, either defending narrow interests or attempting to impose excessively wide regulations. 'On the continent' many Christians had been enthusiastic, and in 1990 the churches in Eastern Europe had just made an influential contribution to the overthrow of Communism, a withdrawal from Russian dominance for which the logical sequel would be membership of the EU – but the British churches, like the British people, still found it hard to cross the Channel with their hearts: Africa could seem nearer than France, let alone Germany.

I was an advocate of Europe as an idea, not necessarily of the euro as a currency. But as I looked at the 12 stars on the new European flag I did think that I saw 12 reasons why Christians could celebrate the project called the construction of Europe.

I had in mind the facts (1) that the peoples of Europe could no longer fight each other for territory and (2) that in their new collaboration power was healthily dispersed between the European institutions. It seemed good and therefore 'of God' that the peoples' standards of living were being raised (3) by the operation of the world's largest market for the sale of goods and services, and (4) by stability in the currency. Firms were now (5) more efficient because of competition and (6) better regulated in the interests of society. But it also seemed good and 'of God' that standards of life outside the market place were being raised by the legal enforcement of (7) basic human rights, (8) the rights of all workers, and (9) the protection of the natural environment. (10) Disadvantaged nations and regions were being brought nearer to equality, (11) help was being given to ease the human costs of the necessary transitions from agriculture to industry and from the old industries to the new technologies, and (12) Western Europe could now afford to be generous to poorer nations in terms of trade and aid, both in its own continent and overseas.

I still think, amid all the problems, that this is the big picture as the proper background to a worthy public discussion of the problems – a debate which has not yet occurred as I write at the beginning of 2002. Moreover, I still think that the churches, which have had a massive involvement in the history of Europe and which still have a substantial presence in every part of the continent, ought to encourage, and make, serious contributions to the debate, using to the full their special opportunities to have fruitful contacts with Christians in other European nations – contacts which can go far deeper than the level of tourism. This is not because the churches have an expertise in economics: it is because the old Europe was both a glory and a scandal as an officially Christian civilization, and the new Europe is best seen as a very imperfect part of the coming of the kingdom of God.

*   *   *

Thus the experience of Westminster taught me quite a lot about the meaning of the kingdom of God for our time, as that transcendently great cause is served both by political activity and in 'civil society' involving activity for the public good outside the sphere of the state. And day by day I was reminded that almost all these activities, when they involve Christians, are the life and work of Christians who are not clergy and who may not spend much time on what is called 'church work'. But I also learned something about the relationship of the Christian churches to this cause which is more important than they are, because I was involved in the work of the British Council of Churches (BCC) and was also made to think about the constitutional connection of Church and State.

At its inauguration in 1942 Archbishop William Temple hoped that the BCC would 'catch the public's imagination and become the channel of new influences' and although after Temple's death the decline in the churches' importance in British life was steep, this council certainly was creative and at least some of the public noticed. Archbishop Geoffrey Fisher called it 'a process, a prophecy, a power' and told one of his biographers (Purcell) that it did its job 'extremely finely' – in a way which kept in touch both with the realities of church life and with the nation's own current problems, 'with a reticence which is right and a sobriety that is necessary'. Archbishop Ramsey paid it his own tribute by paying attention to the business while in the chair and making constructive suggestions. And many leaders of the non-Anglican churches offered the council a similarly significant compliment: amid their responsibilities in their own churches they found time to attend its meetings and its committees and to participate with keen interest. Not all the churches joined but their absence had an advantage, for it left the representatives of those belonging free to develop a strong instrument to do work about which their own consciences agreed.

The BCC became a stimulus to the development of more than 700 local councils and it strenuously advertised and explained the activities of its big brother, the World Council of Churches. It held an annual conference, it met as a full council twice a year outside as well as within the London area, and its special strength lay in the groups which it organized as 'working parties'. Theology could be tackled; there was a creative report on the doctrine of the Holy Trinity, for example. But the most distinctive work was the exploration of areas of national and international life where angels of the churches usually feared to tread. The council did not always endorse what the groups recommended: for example, it objected to the omission from *Sex and Morality* (1966) of the teaching that intercourse is always wrong outside marriage. But the BCC provided a platform for the 'new influences' for which Temple had hoped, and among the new good causes which it supported were welcoming students from overseas plus the much larger number of permanent immigrants from the Commonwealth. Race relations were high on the BCC's agenda years before the nation as a whole woke up to find itself multiracial and multicultural. Later, the council encouraged the English to take seriously pressures for the devolution of power to mini-parliaments in Scotland and Wales. As early as 1965 it sponsored unemotional thinking about *The Future of South Africa*, and four years before Britain 'went into Europe' it was informed about *Christians and the Common Market*. In 1978 *Britain Today and Tomorrow*, by Trevor Beeson, summed up the conclusions of many discussion groups in a project suggested by Archbishop Ramsey. Today it looks very dated, but it has had no successor as a Christian effort.

Inevitably the council faced – and often discussed – problems of its own. The Roman Catholic Church sent 'observers' who participated informally in its work, but talk about full membership which led to the formation of a joint committee in 1967 did not bear fruit. There was some co-operation with Evangelical agencies but not enough. The Scots, Welsh and Irish had their own councils and were active in the BCC, but they could seem far from London. The BCC's member-churches, or at least their national staffs, could complain if the council took more initiatives than they could 'own' and produced more material than they could use. But despite its acknowledged limitations the council could persuade some 500 church leaders to attend a conference in Birmingham for ten days in 1972. With the theme of 'discovering God's will today', it was a conference bombarded by problems; for example, it was the first occasion on which church leaders were seriously confronted by the problems of the deteriorating natural environment. There was realism about the deteriorating churches too, but Archbishop Ramsey was so moved by the honesty that he went around saying that this was the only conference which he had ever believed to be really profitable. In particular he approved of the discussion about prayer in the age of science. I was proud to have suggested it and I wrote an account called *The British Churches Turn to the Future*. That was to seem a stupid title, but it might have been more appropriate if the serious joint thinking begun in 1972 could have had sequels considering the issues of 1982, 1992, 2002 . . . It cannot be maintained that since 1972 urgent problems have been in short supply.

In Lent 1984 the BCC sponsored an ecumenical study programme involving more than a million people, with the theme 'Not Strangers but Pilgrims'. By 1990, however, questions about the council's work, and financial worries about the grants needed (which were not very large), merged with the refusals of the Roman Catholic bishops and Pentecostal pastors to join it as it was then constituted. So the churches which had belonged agreed to replace it by a new start with 'ecumenical instruments' which would have a wider membership. I went to the BCC's farewell conference which was full of optimism.

In the event, local co-operation between the churches grew in the 1990s but it would no doubt have grown anyway: by limited co-operation the churches have had much to gain and nothing to sacrifice. But the 'ecumenical instrument' which was substituted for the BCC at the UK level was starved of finance and became so thin as to be virtually invisible to the public. The plan was that the BCC's commentary on current affairs should be maintained by the churches acting separately yet in consultation with each other, but there were not many noticeable results: before general elections the Roman Catholic bishops, for example, published teaching about *The Common Good* without any substantial consultation with anyone. The best quality of comment was to be found in the weekly Roman Catholic journal the *Tablet*, which was not controlled by that church and had a brilliant editor. An instrument which had built a path for the thoughtful to take through the daunting problems of half a century had been scrapped – at a time when 'think tanks' for social, economic and political analysis were beginning to proliferate in response to the new problems, all more or less ignoring the churches.

Looking back, I find it clear that the decision to scrap the BCC at the UK level was a disservice to the cause of the kingdom of God. The council could have been improved without being abolished. If the decision was taken in order to economize in the churches' resources in personnel and money, it ought to have been remembered more effectively that the cause of a kingdom wider than the churches was the supreme cause of their Lord. If that decision was taken because Roman Catholic and Pentecostal leaders did not wish to take part in the BCC, co-operation between all church leaders at all levels ought to have been encouraged with all possible creativity, but the work done by the BCC in relation to the great, public questions of the day ought to have been continued, perhaps by the creation of an agency ('the Churches' Institute for Social Affairs'?) which churches willing to be sponsors could have used to maintain a service to which they were committed by their faith without being identified with any particular statement of controversial opinion. Such an institute could have relied almost entirely on people willing to contribute from their expertise without being paid. It might also have attracted grants for major projects in the study of problems which concern the community at large. And surely such an institute could be formed in the near future, for the sake of the 'kingdom' which matters most?

*   *   *

It may seem strange if, at a time when the world is in very great danger from war, terrorism, hunger, the misuse of drugs and the pollution of nature, I end this chapter about the kingdom of God with a criticism of the false relationship between Church and State which is reflected in the present establishment of the Church of England. Although the need to crown a new monarch, or to appoint a new archbishop, brings it into the news, this is usually regarded as a subject of no great importance. The rest of the UK is not involved in it and any resentment is mild. Few members of the public are bothered about it; in the General Election of 2001 disestablishment was only a small and little-noticed plank in the platform of the Liberal Democrats. The Established Church no longer troubles anyone who does not belong to it, and that large majority includes many who are rather glad that it is there as a surviving symbol of unity and morality in England, like the monarchy with which it is closely associated. Few of those who actively belong to the Church of England believe that any great scandal is caused by the present system, under which the church decides its doctrine and worship and has a large say in appointments to its leadership. More positively, almost everyone in this church gives a high priority to its commitment to maintain an extensive mission and ministry in the whole nation: every inch of England is in some priest's parish, every parishioner has the right to use the parish church, many communities have a resident pastor, many institutions have a chaplain, a quarter of the nation's primary schools are Church of England schools, plans for 100 new secondary schools have the government's support, the General Synod debates subjects of national interest and sets a tone in church life which is tolerant and broadly comprehensive. So is anything wrong?

As an English Anglican I have to face this question even if it makes others yawn or laugh. A 'no' answer is not so obvious as some other English Anglicans think and research early in 2002 suggests that the majority in this church's active membership has begun to answer 'yes'. This system is unique in the Anglican Communion and unmatched in the rest of the world, and no church in the world would unite with the Church of England except after a change. The system was defended by Paul Avis in *Church, State and Establishment* (2001) but two recent books not in his extensive bibliography told a different tale. In *Public Religions in the Modern World* (1994) José Casanova demonstrated that in democracies pressures on politicians for policies reflecting ethics compatible with religion have a better chance of influencing decisions if they depend on voters' movements rather than on privileges bestowed by the state on the clergy – and where Church and State are not differentiated, the church runs the risk of paying the price which the once powerful church in Spain has paid for its past identification with the Fascism of Franco. Although it used not to be, that is now the official attitude of the Roman Catholic Church. In *Religion and Society in Modern Europe* (1999) René Rémond supplied a history of the slow development towards a consensus that neither Church nor State should dictate to the other. He took his native France as an example of the benefits that can come not only to democracy but also to organized religion (in this case, to the Catholic Church). He regarded England as an inexplicable exception to this sensible rule – and as if to demonstrate its unimportance, this usually careful professor was not fully informed about the actual situation.

The heir to the throne has been among those asking aloud whether the tradition does not need to be updated. While the British currency survives all coins carry reminders that the monarch is 'FD' or 'Defender of the Faith', a title bestowed by the pope on Henry VIII as a reward for a book about the sacraments written largely by Thomas More, but the Prince of Wales suggested that it might be more appropriate to defend 'Faith' less specifically (although not all beliefs deserve defence). The monarch is also the 'Supreme Governor' of the Church of England and it may be asked whether the new diocesan bishops should still take an oath that they hold 'the said bishopric, as well the spiritualities as the temporalities thereof, only of your Majesty' (although the legal meaning of 'spiritualities' is very restricted). The Prime Minister selects names from those nominated by the church for these bishoprics, yet in 1974 the General Synod of the church affirmed by 217 votes to 70 'the principle that the decisive voice should be that of the Church'. As I write, the final decision about who should lead the Church of England and the worldwide Anglican Communion is about to be made by a British politician. Parliament still has the power to veto proposed legislation concerning church life and did so in 1984, by 32 votes to 17 early one morning in the House of Commons. The issue was unimportant but speeches showed that some MPs were using the occasion to attack a church which tolerated views of which they disapproved (the views of David Jenkins, then Bishop of Durham). More seriously, carrying out the decision to make women priests in the 1990s was delayed by nervousness about reaction from Parliament's Ecclesiastical Committee. Yet in an act of 1921 Parliament formally acknowledged the right of the (Presbyterian) Church of Scotland 'to legislate and to adjudicate finally, in all matters of doctrine, worship, government and discipline in the Church' – and in practice few Parliamentarians wish to throw their weight around in the life of the Church of England by imposing their own views in disagreements which are essentially to do with religion (although inevitably Parliament may sometimes be asked to decide uncertainties about church properties by legislation).

In the past (surprisingly, this includes the recent past) there have been some dire predictions about what might follow any tinkering with the familiar system: England, we are warned, might cease to know itself as a basically Christian country. But in reality this is not a danger, since after a long process which reached its climax during the twentieth century the country is already largely secular and, when religious, very varied. The system, so far from being essential to the Christian mission to the nation, is an anachronism which seems defensible to some of the English mainly because it is familiar. The English tend to like conservation of the familiar in areas which do not matter much, and England is psychologically as well as geographically part of an island. But Sweden is another country which does not belong to mainland Europe and which preserves traditions which do not belong to the mainstream of modernity, and it marked the beginning of a new Christian millennium by ending Parliament's control over the national church and in that church that move has been welcomed as an opportunity for renewal with integrity. No one in the world – not even in England – would have dreamed of celebrating AD 2000 by doing the opposite of what has been done in Sweden. In the USA the Catholic Church is the largest church but it is not likely that a president will announce that in order to increase its good influence he will arrange for some of its bishops to be part-time members of the Senate, but will in future appoint them and all their colleagues. No churches in the world can match those of southern Africa in contributions to the national life, but it is not likely that they would expect their influence to be increased by imitation of the arrangements in England.

So it may be realistic to hope that the national mission of the Church of England would continue, and might have more success, if it could be concerned for the welfare and conversion of the whole people without having an image which may have been appropriate in distant days, and I offer a few practical suggestions.

It seems clear that the Coronation of 1953 will never be repeated in that style, which was almost exclusively Anglican, but the ceremony could be made a more convincing affirmation of the legitimacy and good purposes of the state by including welcomes to the new constitutional monarch by political leaders and representatives of many other groups including religions. These could be televised in the magnificently historic Westminster Hall before the monarch crosses the road to Westminster Abbey. The act of worship and dedication solemnized there could still be an Anglican Eucharist, but with as many ecumenical elements as there could be in that context. There would be gratitude among church members, and surely little resentment among others, if the monarch could be the 'senior member' of the Church of England in England, and of the Church of Scotland in Scotland.

The Prime Minister would no longer choose between the nominations for bishoprics, because bishops are essentially pastors and teachers in religion, but the government should of course retain the right to decide who, if anyone, should be summoned to represent this church in the House of Lords, and any such opportunity is of course to be welcomed if the price is not too high. However, the government's plan to reduce the number of bishops in the Lords seems wise, partly because it is doubtful whether all bishops, with more than enough to do, are well equipped to speak and vote on political questions of the day, complex and debatable questions which tend to be resistant to the simplifications of the sermonic style, while the argument that they are equipped to voice the concerns of the local community is flawed since they are not elected to do so in the legislature of a democracy. Fewer bishops may be more authoritative within politics. The expertise of most bishops can be expected to lie more in the field of legislation on ecclesiastical matters, which ought to be removed from Lords and Commons alike, but the advantage of having an 'outside' view of the General Synod could be retained if a voluntary committee of Parliamentarians, with a strong representation of lawyers, could be appointed by the Church to advise the synod about its legislation. Their counsel could not be completely decisive but it could be made public if it was ignored, it could be brought to the notice of Parliament if rejected, and it would surely be taken very seriously.

It would certainly be ridiculous if I ended this chapter about the government of the world by God with a discussion about the future of prayers before parliamentary business. That is a matter which must be decided by Parliament, but whatever the decision Parliament will still be discussing the business of the greater (because divine) 'kingdom'. Also, I see no objection in principle to the right of the Crown to make appointments to a few historic churches of national significance, including Westminster Abbey; that seems a different matter from the appointment of the chief pastor of a diocese by the Prime Minister or the nomination of the pastor of a parish by a private individual as 'patron'. But I can add a hope that a realistic clarification of the current status of the Church of England would strengthen public and official support for the idea of some state aid for religious organizations of all kinds whose aim is to serve the public – in education, in welfare work, in chaplaincies to the forces, the hospitals and the prisons, in the custody of the architectural heritage or in the use of buildings for 'community' purposes. The practice of state aid is already accepted and many grants have already been made without controversy, but there seems to be no philosophy which is a sufficiently clear replacement for the old policy of giving privileges to the Established Church. A church deserves subsidies from taxes only insofar as it clearly serves the cause of the loving government of the world by our non-dictatorial God, always for the sake of the flourishing of the people.

CHAPTER 5

Catholic and New

THE MAIN HOPE for the renewal of the Christian Church for its
mission in the twenty-first century must lie in the Roman
Catholic Church, whose membership outnumbers all the other
churches put together. Around the world it has baptized about a
billion, about a million people belong to its religious orders, it has
about 400,000 priests, and to hundreds of millions the Mass celebrated in this tradition, which has been the school of innumerable
saints in the past, is still the centre of spiritual life.

It may therefore seem strange if I begin this chapter not with the
Second Vatican Council (by far the most important event in the
Christian Church in the twentieth century), and not with thoughts
about possibilities in the future, but with past events in Britain
which had little to do with the event in Rome. I do so because the
failure of hopes in Britain was due to factors which must be taken
seriously in any realistic hopes about renewal anywhere: the Church
that could be could never be built on clouds. And being a witness to
the failure taught me lessons.

In 1958 I wrote a book called *Not Angels but Anglicans*, advo-
cating the reunion of Anglicans, Presbyterians, Methodists and
Congregationalists. It was a minor contribution to what was then a
strong movement. The nature of the unity which was sought was
never precisely defined, but at least it would have involved a great
deal of spiritual 'communion' (not limited to a willingness to accept
one another's ministers as truly ordained and to share Holy Communion in the Eucharist) and a great deal of practical co-operation.
And it was made plain that this process of reunion would gradually
involve a great deal of renewal, meaning in practical terms that
many old prejudices and customs would have to be abandoned for
the sake of the united disciples' mission commanded by Jesus Christ

himself. This unity of Christians serving the kingdom of God would not result in a perfect Church, but it would transform the existing churches and it might well have an impact on the whole religious (or secular) situation in the United Kingdom and on many other places to which the outdated divisions and habits in British Christianity had been exported.

Representatives of the Church of Scotland had recently recommended the introduction of bishops into the Presbyterian system, where the equality of all ordained ministers had been held sacred since the seventeenth century. This was not at the demand of the small Episcopal Church in Scotland: it was in obedience to a wider vision of unity. In England official conversations between Anglicans and Methodists seemed promising: in this year, 1958, a plan was published for 'two parallel churches, side by side, in full communion', moving forward to Stage Two, which would be 'organic unity'. The Church of South India, inaugurated in 1947, had achieved unity between Protestant churches which had come to see that their disunity was a scandal in a predominantly Hindu society. Many Christians elsewhere were seriously considering how to follow this example with modifications. So mission-in-unity could be heard as the music of the future. The clearest pointer to the future seemed to be the World Council of Churches.

Like many others I welcomed this movement towards renewal and reunion because a high amount of unity and of newness is commanded in the New Testament's vision of 'one Lord, one faith, one baptism, one God and Father of all' and in the prayer in the fourth gospel that the disciples 'may all be one . . . that the world may believe'. Paul never refused to argue with his fellow Christians but he began his first letter 'to the church of God that is in Corinth' with the passionate questions: 'Is Christ divided? Was Paul crucified for you?' This seemed to be the challenge to all the churches as the world recovered from the great wars: did the faith which all Christians had in common matter more than the customs which divided them, and was the strength of a more united witness to Christ in neighbourhood and nation more desirable than the conservation of traditions which often had little or no connection with Christian truth? Moreover, I was sure that the essentials treasured by Anglicans would be preserved in the 'Coming Great Church' (a phrase I had picked up from an American book). These essentials were set out in the 'Lambeth Quadrilateral' of 1888: the Catholic scriptures, creeds and sacraments and a 'ministry' ordained by bishops in the 'historical succession'. In common with almost everyone else I assumed that the removal of these safeguards would not be contemplated by Anglicans or by anyone interested in the possibility of a union with them. But of course I also assumed that reunion would involve, for Anglicans as for others, much more than conservation.

I believed that the Church of Scotland and the English Free Churches would be enriched if the Eucharist could be made more obviously the centre of their worship, if their prayer-life could be fed by the Catholic saints, and if they could have the advantage of pastoral care by bishops. The Church of Scotland was in a stronger relationship with its nation than was the Church of England and I hoped that it would become stronger. The English Free Churches did not deserve to be written off (which was the spoken or unspoken attitude of many Anglicans) but I hoped that they would benefit by what the Church of England could contribute: easier access to a whole neighbourhood, more contacts with the decision-makers and (although this could only be whispered) a share in the endowments many of which were inherited from long before the times when 'Dissent' broke away from the Established Church. In particular, many of us were convinced that reunion between Anglicans and Methodists would bring great benefits to both traditions, which ought never to have separated. John and Charles Wesley clearly intended their Methodist societies to be methodical in preaching and practising the Gospel as understood in the tradition of the Church of England, including an emphasis on the Eucharist. The split came not from any disagreement about doctrine or ethics but as a result of Anglican stupidity: parish priests were too often unwilling to give opportunities to Methodist evangelists, and bishops were unwilling to ordain preachers and pastors for America. I knew that disgraceful history; what I did not know was that the Church of England was about to turn its back on Methodism again, encouraging those fellow Christians to decline in numbers since the official response of their church had been to affirm that there was no conclusive reason why they should remain separate.

I also believed that Anglicans would be among those enriched by reunion. Like many others, I wanted the Church of England to be self-governing, with bishops, clergy and laity represented in all big decision-making. I believed that the mission to the unchurched would be strengthened by a more informal style of worship than

Anglicans had so far found congenial: the old insistence on uniformity by unemotional reading out of a book should be replaced, along with the old insistence on royal or parliamentary supremacy in church life. I hoped for the ordination of many unpaid priests somewhat like the Methodist system of local preachers, and for the full use of lay leaders somewhat like the elders in the Presbyterian system. I wanted the congregation to be involved more effectively in the calling of a priest to lead a parish. So many changes seemed to be needed in the Church of England as it existed in 1958.

I did not know that many of these changes would come to pass in a modified fashion without reunion, and also without any infectious excitement, but I did know that in this period many people wanted them as parts of a reconstruction which would open up many possibilities. In 1958 I could quote what Michael Ramsey had written back in 1936:

> While the Anglican Church is vindicated by its place in history, with a strikingly balanced witness to Gospel and Church and sound learning, its greater vindication lies in its pointing through its own history to something of which it is a fragment. Its credentials are its incompleteness, with the tension and travail in its soul. It is clumsy and untidy, it baffles neatness and logic. For it is sent not to commend itself as 'the best type of Christianity', but by its very brokenness to point to the universal Church wherein all have died.

*   *   *

Six years after writing that little book I found myself writing another, in collaboration with a Methodist scholar. It was a report on a conference in Nottingham attended by 329 delegates appointed by the churches belonging to the British Council of Churches and 165 others. This booklet was called *Unity Begins at Home* because this 'First British Conference on Faith and Order' had been planned in order to relate the studies undertaken internationally to the British scene. Some 50,000 booklets had been sold for reading in preparation for it and 10,000 copies were sold of our report. The tone of hopefulness began with a sermon by Archbishop Ramsey, who insisted that the ecumenical movement sprang out of a concern for truth but that it had been learned that 'often when Christian traditions seem far away and repellent to one another it is about the

same things they are caring' and 'beneath any position which seems
to be erroneous there is likely to be some truth to be dug out and recognized'. And he pointed to what had already been found:

> In all our churches we have been looking to the great sources
> and treasure-stores of theology – the Bible, the Fathers, the
> liturgies and so on – to be deepened, corrected, renewed in the
> depth of our grasp. What a change from the days when church-
> es looked to those sources to find weapons to hurl at one
> another!

That conference coincided with the third session of the Second
Vatican Council – the session which produced *Lumen Gentium*, the
most important document yet to emerge from hopes for the Christian future – and in Nottingham prayer for the bishops meeting in
Rome was made in the same spirit of hopefulness. But the concentration was on the churches which belonged to the conference's
sponsoring body, the British Council of Churches. The chairman
was Oliver Tomkins, Bishop of Bristol, who had also been a key
figure in an international 'faith and order' conference, in Lund in
1952, which had challenged the churches to ask themselves very
seriously whether they should not 'act together in all matters except
those in which deep divisions of conviction impel them to act separately'. The Nottingham conference unanimously – and, as it turned
out, creatively – recommended areas where joint action, or at least
much more co-operation, ought to be undertaken: 'learning together
(including local ecumenical study conferences), lay training, youth
work, children's work, men's and women's organizations, local
church publications, Christian Aid to help the world's poor, pro-
grammes of visiting, concern for, and service to, the whole life of the
local and wider community'. Equally creative was the idea that the
time had come for 'local ecumenical projects' in the shape of buildings shared by more than one denomination as the home of a
fellowship exploring new ways of 'being the church'. But the resolu-
tion which attracted most attention looked beyond such
co-operation. 'United in our urgent desire for One Church renewed
for mission, this conference invites the member churches of the
British Council of Churches, in appropriate groupings such as
nations, to covenant together to work and pray for the inauguration
of union by a date agreed amongst them. We dare to hope that this

date should be not later than Easter 1980.' Only five votes were cast against adopting the first sentence and only 53 against the hope for 1980.

It was a deliberately provocative hope and it soon began to look absurdly over-optimistic: so far from the churches agreeing to reunion by 1980, there has not been a Second British Conference on Faith and Order which might have been more realistic. But I have always regarded the complete disappointment as a tragedy. Admittedly the tone of refusal was set by the Church of Scotland, whose General Assembly had thrown out the proposal for bishops in 1959. But ten years later the representatives of the Anglican clergy and laity in England failed to produce the 75 per cent majority required for the acceptance of Anglican/Methodist reunion. Only the House of Bishops produced the two-thirds majority needed in each House and the overall majority was only 66 per cent. Disagreement concentrated on the proposed 'service of reconciliation' during which hands would have been laid on the heads of Anglican and Methodist ministers alike with the prayer that the Holy Spirit might be given to each according to his need, but in a referendum more than a third of the Church of England's clergy had indicated that they would be unwilling to take part in such a service.

Not only Anglicans were opposed. In the 1890s some leading Methodists had raised their voices among those calling for a United Free Church, but Methodism had not sat alongside other 'Nonconformists' in a single national council (the Free Church Federal Council) until 1937 and no United Free Church has ever proved possible. Reunion with the Church of England could be held to offer even greater dangers in this nation at a time when Methodists outnumbered Anglicans around the world, partly because of their strength in the USA. In the USA Methodism had powerful bishops, but to be asked in England to 'take episcopacy into the system' (like a pill?) before being welcomed to receive communion at Anglican altars could seem an exhibition of the Establishment's arrogance. So the Voice of Methodism was a movement of protest against the reunion scheme. But this opposition won the votes of a little less than a quarter of the Methodist Conference (the governing body) and conservatism was stronger in the Church of England.

Its most distinguished spokesman was Archbishop Fisher, who had made the suggestion about other churches taking episcopacy in a sermon of 1946 which had restarted the talk about reunion. Now

Fisher was retired but that did not stop him campaigning in the conviction that greater unity should not mean any radical change in the Established Church which he had left (as he claimed) orderly and 'in good heart'. He did not mind disagreeing with his successor, Ramsey (partly because he had once been Ramsey's headmaster), and his leadership of the opposition strengthened its destructive power – without halting the decline of the Established Church.

A rather different form of opposition by conservatives came from some Anglican Evangelicals. They might have been expected to desire teamwork in evangelism with the heirs of John and Charles Wesley but at that stage their conservatism could take the form of nostalgia for the days when James I had been a royal theologian in the Calvinist tradition and the Church of England had been more exclusively Protestant, with the Book of Common Prayer and the Thirty-Nine Articles defining the enforced standards of worship and doctrine. They could lament the disappearance of that uniformity but value the far less uniform Church of England which they knew as 'a good boat to fish from' (for souls), despite its many leaks. They saw little point in unity with the Methodists, who, they reckoned, had been infected by a decadent liberalism even more than present-day Anglicans: it was said that a union would end up as 'two corpses in one coffin'. Those very defensive attitudes were being modified during the 1960s but they were in the background to reactions to the Anglican/Methodist scheme. More publicly it was now argued that the proposed 'service of reconciliation' might be interpreted as a denial that Methodist ministers were already ordained. They declared that this possibility troubled their consciences although the Methodist Conference produced a majority of 76 per cent in favour of the plan.

In contrast, Anglo-Catholics could object that the proposed service 'reconciling' Methodist ministers with the Church of England did not make it sufficiently plain that it was an ordination which one day Roman Catholics might accept. Yet previously the Lambeth Conference of Anglican bishops had argued that a service of reconciliation would be needed, and the Church of South India had been criticized severely for not holding one during its formation; and presumably any such service would always be open to different interpretations by those being reconciled. Indeed, the ordinations of the Church of England itself were already wide open to rival theologies. Thus Anglo-Catholic opponents of the plan were demanding a clarification which Anglicans had been unable to achieve in their own diversity, resulting in the official verdict of the Roman Catholic Church (delivered in 1896 and in 2002 not yet formally cancelled) that Anglican ordinations were 'absolutely null and utterly void'.

What happened in the next few years showed that the rejection by conservatives in 1969 had been decisive. The English scheme was brought back in 1972 – a move which was not unreasonable, since the opposition had come from minorities giving different reasons which might have been answered after reflection – but the majorities in the newly reconstituted General Synod of the Church of England were again insufficient. Speeches by Archbishop Ramsey on both occasions were eloquent but in the event not sufficiently convincing. On 3 May 1972 I had the experience of seeing how moved he was when presiding at a Eucharist with many prayers and hymns about Christian unity. The service in St Margaret's, Westminster, might have been the prelude to a great act of reunion – but before that day was over he was speaking in public about being in spiritual darkness.

The advocates of visible and fairly rapid reunion summoned up the courage for other efforts. Five months after this defeat the United Reformed Church was formed by most of the Congregationalists and Presbyterians in England, and in the climate created by this inauguration (in Westminster Abbey) it was proposed that this new body, together with the Anglican and Methodist Churches, should make a 'covenant' to seek reunion. Such a covenant was actually made in Wales, where in the early years of the century relationships between the churches had been bitter, and in England a plan suggested that the URC and the Methodists should have bishops and should explore with the Anglicans 'further steps to make more clearly visible the unity of all Christ's people'.

Again a reunion plan failed to attract an adequate majority in the General Synod of the Church of England. In 1982 only two of the 38 bishops were opposed but the main objections came from Anglo-Catholics led by Graham Leonard, then Bishop of London but later a Roman Catholic. The Houses of Bishops and of Laity agreed but the majority in the House of Clergy fell short by 5 per cent of the two-thirds required. The inclusion of the URC could cause a special problem, partly because not all the 'moderators' in their 'districts' were to become bishops, but more significant was the fact that Pope John Paul II had visited England only a month before, in an atmosphere of euphoria: it could seem crazy to bother about the URC, or about Methodism, if the road to reunion with Rome was about to be opened. That was only a possibility, but to some it seemed to deserve the sacrifice of an actual plan – a plan which would not have destroyed the wider hope of reconciliation with Rome.

*   *   *

That long process which consumed the energies of many Christians had few tangible results, in my view because the chief mistake made was not to proclaim loudly enough that a large measure of reunion is indeed important for the Christian mission in the modern world. 'Unity' and 'mission' have been joined in countless statements by churches as well as individuals but there has not been a strong enough vision of what is to be gained after the sacrifices.

Some true points are made by fellow Christians who take the view that 'unity schemes' harm the cause of Christianity. It is correctly pointed out that the attachment of regular churchgoers to the churches as they exist is a solid reality with which wise leaders and pastors must reckon. It is also said that the faithful are now usually willing to accept other Christians as fellow Christians and to support local co-operation when that seems practical and does not interfere too much with existing loyalties. And the further point is made that styles of worship, spirituality and theology have become less rigid almost everywhere, so that Christians who are nourished mainly by their own traditions may use other sources; occasionally they may even receive Holy Communion together, with or without official encouragement. The theological positions which meant that most Anglicans would not practise 'intercommunion' with non-Anglicans until reunion had been achieved have been abandoned one by one in my lifetime. Defenders of those positions used to argue that they were needed if reunion was to seem important, and maybe they have been proved right. Finally, enthusiasts for reunion need to face the fact that it does not automatically bring numerical growth; instead, those who dissent from the union may survive better than those who unite. The reunion which produced the United Reformed Church in 1972 did not produce growth: in the next 20 years its membership was halved, in keeping with the Church of England's own decline.

All that is true – but it is also, and much more importantly, true that in their continuing separation all the British churches have become increasingly absorbed in the problems of survival with decreasing resources in people and money. Evangelism has been seen to be a necessity but it is also the case that such evangelism as there has been has not produced widespread enthusiasm for the churches: largely, the conversions have been to Christ as the saviour of the person, not to a religious institution which seems to live in the past. And divisions which use Christian labels have remained a scandal: there ought to be no argument about that in a United Kingdom which includes Northern Ireland. Not enough interest is taken in the churches by the public to produce a general outrage about their divisions, but instead there is boredom. Whether or not they become Christians, very few modern people are fascinated by the issues which divided Christians in circumstances very different from those of the present day (Luther or Henry VIII against the Papacy of the Renaissance, Wesley against the complacent clergy of the eighteenth century, etc.). Nor are many people fascinated when people belonging to one denomination are officially allowed to 'receive communion' from a minister ordained in another denomination; to them, it seems to be a permission long overdue. But they might be more interested in 'One Church renewed for mission' – a mission reaching them. At any rate, come high water or low water, the ecumenical voyage into the future has begun and Christians have no good reason to abandon it. The destination was stated by the Lambeth Conference of bishops back in 1888:

> We must set before us the Church of Christ as He would have it, one spirit and one body, enriched in all those elements of divine truth which the separated communities of Christians now emphasise severally, strengthened by the interaction of all those gifts and graces which our divisions now hold asunder, filled with all the fullness of God.

It seems very unlikely that such a Church will emerge easily out of Christians coming together locally, without bothering about the national level at which theology is debated and regulations and budgets are made. Of course local experiments can be very fruitful, for example the sharing of church buildings, but they soon run up against limits. That lesson ought to have been learned permanently in 1970, when the Anglo-Catholic Graham Leonard joined with the Evangelical leader James Packer, and two others who ought to have known better, to produce an alternative plan for *Growing into Union*. Their proposal was that the Church should unite area by area instead of nationally, apparently ignoring the difficulties which would arise from the fact that Anglicans and Methodists alike were in strong national organizations – and the united churches were to have 'presbyters' who were to be 'accepted' by their bishops, avoiding any argument about a service of reconciliation but apparently forgetting the passionate Anglo-Catholic objections to this method when it had been put into effect in South India. The response to this diversionary but unrealistic plan was therefore dismissive almost everywhere, and since then the experience of 'local ecumenical projects' which go beyond co-operation has been to a large extent one of frustration. If these projects, now renamed partnerships, are to move towards the churches' reunion by doing almost everything together, they are not really connected with churches which remain complacently divided – but if the partnership amounts to little more than the sharing of a building, it does not offer much of a vision of the world Church's future.

Nor was such a vision clear and strong in the report published in 2001 after long conversations between representatives of the Church of England and the Methodist Church. It registered a welcome affirmation that both churches already belong to the 'One, Holy, Catholic and Apostolic Church of Jesus Christ' and that all their ministers already 'possess Christ's commission given through the Church'. If these agreements are endorsed by the churches concerned, they will indeed be steps 'on the way to the full, visible unity of Christ's Church'. But no service of reconciliation was recommended at this stage, since for most practical purposes the proposed covenant would leave the two churches divided. They would 'take account of each other's concerns' and 'bring about closer collaboration' with a joint commission to encourage 'implementation', but their commitment would be limited to that, their ministries would not be 'interchangeable' between the churches, and any 'eucharistic sharing' would be 'in accordance with the rules of our respective churches'. The excitement which had accompanied earlier plans for changes which could have been noticed by the public seemed to have died down, and this report's very cautious tone did not promise that the new hopes would swiftly burst into the flame of renewal for a united mission.

I find that I must compare the defeats of 1969, 1972 and 1982 with those of 1660–62 and 1688–89, going back beyond the defeat of the Wesleys' hope that their mission to the nation might be allowed to operate within the Church of England. Twice in the seventeenth century, after the civil war when a king had been executed and after a crisis when a king had been deposed and exiled, there was a chance to reconcile Anglicans with other Christians in an enlarged Church of England, making that church more worthy of its name. On each occasion the chance was thrown away by the conservatism of many of the Anglican clergy, who refused to allow enough liberty of interpretation to other Christians (the Puritans) who were willing to serve alongside them in a national church which would preserve and preach the essentials. On the second occasion Dissenters were granted toleration, although not full civil rights. However, the division was not healed between the privileged church and what developed into Victorian Nonconformity – and in the period 1814–1914 bitterness between 'church' and 'chapel' certainly did great harm both to the nation and to the churches. Both the nation and the churches grew in those years but there could be no escape from an old fact: if the world cannot see that Christians really love one another to an extent which surprises the world, the world will not believe.

Can the failures of 1969, 1972 and 1982 be put right? I do not know. But I know that they were wrong and were the fault of the Church of England. Of course the opponents of the proposals were following their consciences, but good reasons can be given for thinking them mistaken.

*   *   *

The failure of reunion plans which came remarkably near to success has forced many who supported them, including me, to think again. We have seen that, to be realistic, hopes for the future must include three essentials: a diversity even greater than was found to be necessary in the Church of South India must be accepted without grudging, in a prolonged Stage One and in the union which must be Stage Two; both Roman Catholicism and the Evangelical movement must be taken far more seriously than was the case in the plans which failed; and the basis must be not diplomacy aiming to reconcile old traditions without much change but the common acknowledgement of what is now seen to be true and right. The ecumenical voyage will therefore be far more difficult than we imagined in the 1950s or 1960s, when it was the constant tendency of the ecumenical movement (at least in its councils of churches, theological commissions and official publications) to stress existing agreements, based as these seemed to be both on Scripture and on Tradition. It may be found relevant if, reluctantly, I now tell a little of the story of how I was made to think more deeply about the urgency of new thinking in the churches – and about the sad necessity which many Christians now feel to make up their own minds and take their own actions, hoping that one day churches and consciences will move together.

In 1978 I was appointed by the Crown as Dean of Norwich Cathedral, one of the loveliest of all the great churches in England, surrounded by a Close which was in effect an exceptionally handsome village of the Jane Austen era. The cathedral was regarded by most of the county of Norfolk as its proud symbol, and it had recently been given a new vigour in its life by an imaginative and energetic dean. Indeed, I was assured that so much activity had been started, and would be sustained, that fewer initiatives might be in order. I was encouraged to continue to work as an author and journalist, so I began a history of Christian England in three volumes. And I found other delights. The cathedral's worship was an inspiration; its supporters supported me; the clergy of a mainly rural diocese invited me to visit their parishes and even expressed some interest in what I could say in those tranquil scenes.

However, it was in Norwich that I experienced the agony of divorce after a period of legal separation. I shall not be expected to discuss here why our marriage broke down, but it will be relevant if I admit that it made me reconsider what I had written in a book of 1962 called *This Church of England*, published by that church. I had written that

> according to the Prayer Book, marriage is ended on earth only by death itself. Here are the words: 'till death us do part'. These words are based on what Jesus taught. No words could be clearer. In the eyes of the Church, the failure of a Christian marriage must be a sin as well as a tragedy. People should not expect to be remarried in church. If divorced people do remarry, they ought not to receive Holy Communion without asking the bishop. The bishop will advise them about when and how they may be restored to the Church's full fellowship.

Because I still thought that the tradition of permanent marriage ought to guide my own life, I tried frantically to avert or retrieve the disaster, as those who shared the pain with me would, I think, testify, and when I failed I thought that my future would be one of sorrow and loneliness, perhaps also of no work which I could enjoy, although I was to do what I could for our four children. But the authorities of the Church did not ask me to resign; instead, in due course they gave me a fresh start by moving me to another cathedral. This was in Southwark, amid South London's problems which were very different from the delights of Norfolk.

I moved there without a thought of a second marriage but while I was back in London I was totally surprised to learn from a mutual friend that Sybil, who had been a missionary in South Africa for more than 20 years, was willing to take me on. When to that miracle were added the joys of seeing the children rebuild their own lives, and of having colleagues and friends as good as those in Norwich, the 11 years in Southwark, followed by retirement in beautiful Winchester, became the best time of my life. And I am sure that many others have experienced a second marriage, or some other new start in life, as God's blessing.

But was what we did contrary to the plain teaching of the Bible and to the mind of the Church? Did we defy those authorities for merely selfish reasons? My colleagues and congregation in Southwark allowed Sybil (who had not been married before) and me to be married in the context of a Eucharist, and their support was appreciated all the more because in this same period, 1984–85, the General Synod of the Church of England showed itself to be unable to make up its mind about such weddings. The argument had been rumbling for years but had become public in 1972. The synod had then debated a report which advocated a change in the regulations passed by the Convocation of the Clergy most recently in 1957, against the marriage of a divorced person in church during the lifetime of a former partner. That debate was inconclusive. Another commission presented another report with the same recommendation six years later, producing other debates in the national and diocesan synods which again proved inconclusive: the majority accepted that some marriages after a divorce could rightly take place in a church, but there was no agreement about how to authorize them.

This confusion was a reflection of a real division of convictions within the Church of England. One group believed that a valid marriage is indissoluble: as is well known, this is the Roman Catholic Church's doctrine although a first marriage may be pronounced not to have been valid. Another group believed that a second marriage might be permitted but that it must be a 'civil' one, before a registrar appointed by the state, and the Church should allow only a service of 'blessing'. Others believed that the vows of lifelong fidelity could be taken again within a (simplified) church wedding, provided that an inquiry involving people outside the parish had investigated the circumstances of the breakdown of the first marriage and the motives behind the new one. And a fourth group believed that a church wedding could be right for some applicants but that the decision should be made in the parish. Sybil and I very much wanted our union to be a part of our church life and would have been happy to submit to a formal inquiry but even without knowing that we should have had to wait until the next century we felt that we had no duty to wait until the General Synod had made up its mind. We wanted to live together and I needed help rather urgently. So ours became one of the large number of church weddings granted to couples with this problem as a local decision, with no full authorization but with our superiors not exercising a veto; in fact they could not have been kinder. In 2002, almost all the dioceses of the Church of England have agreed in principle that some divorcees should be allowed to marry again in church – but again without agreement about the procedure.

Had I been a Roman Catholic this second marriage would have meant that I was no longer allowed to receive Holy Communion, and as soon as I knew that my first marriage (which certainly had existed, producing a family) had died, of course I wondered whether I could still function as a priest presiding at Holy Communion in the Church of England. Since I was not sacked this seemed to be a question for my own conscience. I had been given a Bible at the time of my ordination 'to the office and work of a priest in the Church of God' (the bishop had written those solemn words in it) and now I had to 'wrestle with the Scriptures' (in the old phrase). When I did, I found an intensely personal significance in the evidence which had influenced the two commissions reporting to the Church of England.

I had been persuaded by those commissions at the time that remarriage for someone else might be right in some circumstances, without realizing how much the matter was going to mean to me.

For the fact was that the Church of England's very strict official line was out of keeping with most of the rest of Christian understanding of the relevance of the Bible. The Roman Catholic Church has a procedure whereby a first marriage can be 'annulled', stating that it had never been a true Christian marriage. Most Protestant churches, and even the very conservative Orthodox churches, allow a second marriage after a divorce unless there is a special cause for scandal. And in the New Testament the question was not answered as simply as I had claimed in 1962.

The teaching of Jesus seems to have been limited to the single point on which there must be agreement between all Christians: the breakdown of any marriage is contrary to the will of God, despite the provision for divorce made in the Hebrew Bible. In Mark's gospel I read the words once again: 'A man shall leave his father and mother and be joined to his wife and the two shall become one flesh . . . therefore what God has joined together, let no one separate' (10.7–9). I was still sure that these words stated the Christian vision of marriage. Indeed, my own recent experience had only confirmed my conviction and in the years to come, when I was to see other marriages come to grief, the certainty was to be further strengthened. But I saw that these solemn and clear words had to be connected with human tragedies. In this gospel, which tradition said was written in Rome, the teaching was applied to divorces initiated by wives, as was possible under Roman but not under Jewish law: 'if a wife divorces her husband and marries another, she commits adultery' (10.12). But Matthew concentrated on what seems to have been a practice which was frequent among the Jews in Palestine: a man might divorce his wife simply because he wanted another partner, often younger. This practice deserved severe condemnation but the wife who had been rejected, or the husband who had been rejected by the wife's adultery, deserved sympathy. So in the Sermon on the Mount, which is not a mandate for promiscuity, it is written that 'whoever divorces his wife, except for unchastity [the almost certain meaning of the Greek *porneia*], and marries another commits adultery' (5.32 and 19.9). In his first letter to them Paul allowed the Corinthians to regard a marriage as over 'if the unbelieving partner separates': in such a case the Christian 'is not bound' for 'it is to peace that God has called you' (7.15). A new marriage appears to be allowed since to be married was regarded as a normal part of 'peace' although this is not definitely stated. Paul knew that 'the Lord' had not made this allowance, but evidently he thought it a Christian thing to say for pastoral reasons in this situation.

It is noticeable that he did not mention adultery as making an exception to a rule, any more than the Sermon on the Mount mentioned desertion: evidently there was no intention to legislate with rules covering all situations. Nor, indeed, was it Matthew's intention to present the Sermon on the Mount as a code of law. It was no legislator who taught that 'if a man looks at a woman with a lustful eye, he has already committed adultery with her in his heart. If your right eye causes your downfall, tear it out and fling it away!' (5.28, 29). Although obviously I am not objective, I am therefore one of those who believe that in some circumstances a marriage after divorce can be defended after a study of Scripture and Tradition as well as after personal experience. But the experience has made me share the unhappiness of many divorced and remarried, but officially excommunicated, members of the Roman Catholic Church, to which I now turn.

*   *   *

The visit of John Paul II to Britain in the summer of 1982 (the only time when a pope in office has visited this island) came when this country was about to go to war with Argentina and a message about peace coming from Rome could not fail to move Christian hearts. As the pope and archbishop knelt together in prayer in Canterbury Cathedral many such hearts must have been moved to feel something of the potential force of the papacy's unifying role, gathering and guiding both churches and nations. It would be a great advance in the coming of the kingdom of God if essential Christianity could at last have one universally respected spokesperson, and if the world could have a moral leader, carrying weight by prestige – and history has given the Bishop of Rome a unique vocation to perform that service to the servants of God. On other occasions during the pontificate of John Paul II such a future has seemed to be arriving: one example was the meeting of leaders of the major religions under his presidency in Assisi in 1986, assembled in order to pray together and together face the social and environmental problems of our planet.

But in some very important ways the time when John Paul II has been pope has increased the problems. In 1994 *The Catechism of the Catholic Church* was published in English and was commended by him as a comprehensive and authoritative statement of 'what the Catholic Church believes'. I therefore wrote an Anglican response with the title *What is Catholicism*? It was not an attack on the pope or his church: it included quite a long, and certainly sincere, chapter on the 'true glory' of Catholicism and although it went on to offer criticisms it was reviewed in the Catholic *Tablet* by a leading American Catholic theologian, Richard McBrien, who made the criticism that I did not seem to realize how many Catholics would agree with almost the whole of my position.

I addressed a preface 'to an unknown pope' because it seemed not unreasonable to believe that in the future there would be further progress in understanding and reconciliation. I could point to the striking changes in what could be seen and heard in the average Catholic church, the altar now close to the people, the priest no longer muttering in Latin, the images of Mary and other saints no longer rivalling the Saviour . . . And I could appeal to the more theoretical agreements already reached by the Anglican/Roman Catholic International Commission. These covered subjects which had been ferociously disputed in the past.

There had been passionate Protestant objections to doctrines taught in the Middle Ages and reaffirmed in the Tridentine Profession of Faith (1564). Because it is the Church's right to judge 'the true meaning and interpretation of Sacred Scripture', and because the pope has 'infallible teaching authority', it was taught that 'in the Mass a true, proper and propitiatory sacrifice is offered to God on behalf of the living and the dead, with changes of the whole substance of the bread into the body of Christ and of the wine into his blood'. But now it could be agreed that Christ's self-sacrifice is represented with spiritual power when he unites his people to himself, and thus to his sacrifice of himself, by being spiritually present in the consecrated bread and wine. Since the heart of Christian 'priesthood' is presidency at the Eucharist, agreement about the significance of ordination can follow. So can agreement about our 'justification' and 'salvation' through the 'grace' of God received through 'faith' or trust in God, enabling entry into the 'people of God', a 'royal priesthood' which is spiritually washed and fed by the great sacraments.

Similarly, there can be agreement about Mary. Developing Catholic doctrines had seemed to Protestants to lift her out of humanity, teaching that she was without 'original' or 'personal' sin, that she was 'assumed' body and soul into heaven, that she was 'queen of heaven' and the 'mediatrix' of divine grace. But it can now be agreed that divine grace prepared her to be the mother of the Saviour, and that she now shares his eternal glory; and it can be hoped that this agreement would be enough to make unity possible in humble obedience to God's will.

It is sadly significant, however, that the Vatican's official response has been to ask for further clarifications in order to make sure that any agreement would not be disloyal to its past teachings, and these teachings have been reiterated without revision in a number of statements made or authorized by John Paul II. That reaction has reminded Anglicans how difficult it is to agree about the authority of the Roman Catholic *magisterium*, a term which in current usage means the pope and the other bishops but which used to include theologians. Many issues arise in church life but inevitably the public is most interested in questions to do with the ethics of sexuality and its consequences, and the answers to such questions cannot consist of statements which are diplomatically evasive or ambiguous: in this field one either does something or one does not. Here as elsewhere divisions may look deep, yet already many Roman Catholics believe that the official positions restated in the catechism of the 1990s ought not to be decisive or permanent.

This has been shown in many surveys of Catholic opinion and by the voting in countries, traditionally Catholic, where laws embodying what is still the official Catholic teaching have been repealed as being unsuitable in a modern democracy. Even for devout Catholics things have changed: thus Bernard Häring changed the title of a treatise on Catholic ethics from *The Law of Christ* (1955) to *Free and Faithful in Christ* (1978). Many Roman Catholics are now among the Christians who think that moral decisions should be based not on a timeless general law, divine or natural, but on the love shown by Christ being applied within a personal or political situation; not on laws which are rigid because the Church thinks that such firmness is good for its own power but on careful conclusions made in the best interests of the people affected; and not on rules laid down by authorities who are outside the situation (who are not married, for example) but on results known by the experience of the people involved. This does not mean that no reference need be made to the New Testament or to moral principles, but it does mean that the teaching of Jesus about behaviour appropriate to the kingdom of

God was a vision of perfection; it was not legislation. It also means that principles are not Christian principles if they are not humane.

*   *   *

In Britain one marriage in every five currently ends in divorce and an unknown number of couples live together without marriage partly because they would not want a legal divorce to add to the pain of the possible end to their relationship. In the catechism it is taught that a union after a divorce cannot be recognized as valid because it 'objectively contravenes God's law' and that those who seek reconciliation with the church through the sacrament of penance must commit themselves to living in 'complete continence'. But I need not comment further. Much the same is taught about the use of artificial contraception within marriage; any such act is 'intrinsically evil' and 'a falsification of the inner truth of conjugal love'. In 1983 the leading professor of Christians ethics in the USA, Charles Curran, was deprived of his post in the Catholic University of America after unwillingness to echo this teaching, which according to recent polls is rejected by more than 80 per cent of Catholics in the USA.

This total prohibition is based not on Scripture (where the subject is not mentioned) but on the argument that nature condemns sexual acts not 'open to the transmission of life'. Yet for most humans of a suitable age it seems natural to desire to be sexually active whether or not the time is potentially fertile, and this is particularly the case within a happy union with a partner. Indeed, this catechism itself states that marriage is intrinsically good and that sexual acts during infertile periods 'encourage tenderness'. In the experience of the married, however, confinement to infertile periods is in practice unreliable, and also unhelpful if the consummation of love has to be postponed. And although the encouragement of breeding is one of the uses of sex, nature has clearly decreed that since Earth's resources are limited, so the population must also be kept in check, by famine if necessary. So it can seem obviously sensible to limit the production of children and if that frustrates nature we can remember that nature is frustrated every day by medicine and surgery, and even by the wearing of clothes.

In strongly traditional societies conservatively masculine attitudes are of course often applied to marriage, but many studies of Catholic opinion have suggested that most married couples with equality between the woman and the man and with access to artificial methods of contraception use them with a clear conscience. Indeed, a change to a realistic position was recommended by 58 of the 62 members of the commission appointed to examine the question before Pope Paul VI issued *Humanae Vitae* in 1968, a document which reaffirmed traditional teaching and which more than any other pronouncement in history destroyed the credibility of the 'teaching church' in the eyes of this church's own membership. It is now widely agreed that together with the excommunication of remarried Catholics who now desire to be faithful, this ban on artificial contraception within marriage must be removed in the necessary renewal of Roman Catholicism. It has done immense damage – to the health of many women, to the happiness of many marriages and to the vitally needed limitation of the world's population as well as to the Church itself, for example in discouraging the laity from consulting the clergy about moral issues. But this attempt by the few to pile heavy burdens on the shoulders of the many (Matthew 23.4) is being nullified by the consciences of the many who learn about marriage by being married.

In addition to the use of artificial contraception other sexual activities are condemned as being contrary to natural law and therefore to 'God's law' – although this catechism grants that 'the precepts of the natural law are not perceived by everyone clearly and immediately' and Jeremy Bentham was more naughty than wrong to call natural law 'nonsense on stilts'. For example, it is taught that masturbation is 'an intrinsically and gravely disordered action' – although it is no longer called a 'mortal' sin which can lead to 'unending punishment' in hell if it was committed knowing that it is 'malicious' but not included in repentance before death (as was taught in an official American catechism, curiously called *The Teaching of Christ*, in 1984).

To most people it would seem far more important that homosexual acts are condemned as 'intrinsically disordered': they are, it is said, 'contrary to the natural law' and are presented in Scripture as 'acts of grave depravity'. At the Lambeth Conference of 1998, 389 of the Anglican bishops agreed on rejecting homosexual practice as 'incompatible with Scripture' and probably most Anglicans who are regular churchgoers would agree with them. In most other churches the situation seems to be much the same. But it may be doubted whether this attitude will persist as the knowledge spreads that a fully homosexual orientation is not curable. The Vatican maintained that it is as recently as 1975, but scientific and medical opinion over-whelmingly agrees that it is in fact natural for a minority – a minority which has been large in the histories of church leadership and artistic creativity. This catechism of the 1990s claims that the 'psychological genesis' of the condition 'remains largely unex-plained' but it does recognize that people with this unexplained condition deserve a sensitive respect. It seems possible that when there is more acceptance of the scientific explanation of this condi-tion – as being no less natural than the colour of hair – the moral acceptance of some acts will follow when the homosexuals con-cerned do not have the rare (but admirable) vocation to celibacy or 'singleness'.

There should be no need for this second acceptance to be held up by a belief that the teaching of Scripture on this matter is all time-lessly authoritative. (Presumably the 190 Anglican bishops who voted against the 389 did not believe this.) No Christian need accept the law that those guilty of this 'abomination' must be 'cut off' (Leviticus 18.22, 29) and no educated Christian need be blind to the fact that Paul mistakenly thought that all homosexual activity was perverted, not natural (Romans 1.24–27). It seems preferable to notice the report that Jesus said that some men are incapable of a sexual relationship with a woman 'because they were born so' (Matthew 19.12), while not claiming that this passage of Scripture decides the current disagreement between Christians. The issue ought to be settled by combining the New Testament's moral vision taken as a whole with modern knowledge of the facts and with modern (or postmodern) sensitivity to minorities.

It seems clear that homosexual practice is imperfect, for the rela-tionship cannot be strengthened by the natural desire to bring up children in a stable family where both mother and father are meant to be carers and models. Heterosexual acts between the unmarried are also imperfect even when they are loving not promiscuous, because they cannot be a kind of sacrament for a socially recognized and affirmed commitment to stay together in love until death. However, it seems both true and significant that in many parts of the world many people, including Christians, perform such acts repeat-edly, with untroubled consciences and with the approval or toleration of most other people who are sexually active. And the use of condoms seems to most people positively moral. It greatly reduces the risk of making unwanted babies while making love – and it fights the spread of sexually transmitted diseases including the very terrible epidemic of AIDS. In 1991 the bishops of the Church of England corporately expressed support for lay homosexuals who have conscientiously chosen 'a loving and faithful partnership, in intention lifelong, where mutual self-giving includes the physical expression of their attachment'. They offered no such support to homosexual clergy, pointing out that by tradition 'certain possibilities are not open to the clergy by comparison with the laity', but that distinction in matters of morality between clergy and laity has become a matter for debate. There will always be a need for discretion by and about gay clergy in particular, and there will always be a duty of care and discipline to be exercised by those called to be pastors of pastors, but the controversy about homosexuality in general will probably end like the dispute about contraceptives, allowed to Anglicans by a Lambeth Conference in 1930 after many years of resistance.

Is the termination of a pregnancy always to be utterly condemned? When used as birth control it is obviously a far worse evil than the activities so far mentioned in this section. There is therefore a much wider respect for the 'pro-life' stand taken here by the Roman Catholic leadership, and the only question which most Christians will think it right to ask is whether there are any circumstances in which abortions by modern procedures may be the lesser of two evils. Once again nature's 'law' is less clear than may be thought: natural miscarriages occur in a fifth (at least) of all human pregnancies, often after genetic malfunctioning. Also, the Catholic Church's tradition is more ambiguous: this catechism teaches that 'the embryo, like any other human being, must be treated as a person from conception' (the logical consequence being that very many millions now in eternity lived on earth as embryos) – yet in 1566 the Roman Catechism taught that 'according to the order of nature the rational soul is united with the body only after a certain lapse of time' and in the Middle Ages Thomas Aquinas thought that the foetus is ensouled only at 40 days for a boy and 90 for a girl. Current medical opinion is that a foetus, always a person potentially, becomes capable of mental activity at 40 days approximately, and independent life at 28 weeks. Another factor is that legalized abortions with modern surgery inflict far less physical damage on mothers than did abortions in the past. Also, counselling is now available, rather than criminalization. It seems that a Christian may be 'pro-life' without being totally anti-abortion when the pregnancy is still in its early stages and there are tragedies such as rape, crippling malformation or serious danger to a mother's physical or mental health. And polls have shown that this is in fact the moral position now taken by large numbers of Christians, including many Roman Catholics.

*　　　　*　　　　*

Questions about the authority of the papacy can also be acute in church life, since reasons of conscience are given when papal jurisdiction is rejected not only by Protestants and Anglicans but also by the strongly conservative Eastern Orthodox. In order to give a recent example of consciences being obeyed against strong advice from Rome, I briefly summarize an experience in South London, when a development which seemed to many of us utterly right was condemned by the papacy (and in this case, also by the Eastern Orthodox): the ordination of women as priests.

For Christmas 1982 I moved with my children into an area which was more or less derelict, although it had a splendid view of St Paul's Cathedral across the river. Behind our new home was a ruined soap factory; to the left was an abandoned power station; to the right was a site empty since the bombing and now used as a depot for rubbish collection; beyond that were disused warehouses; and we could just hear the sound of bells from Southwark Cathedral, obviously in need of a good wash and a great deal of new money. But during my time there, or soon after it, came what is called 'urban regeneration'. Residents in many new houses and flats now enjoyed the riverside; the new Tate Gallery of modern art was housed magnificently in the old power station; Shakespeare's Globe Theatre was reconstructed where the rubbish carts had been, near its original site; and the generosity of its friends enabled the cathedral to acquire a new cleanliness and new buildings fit to be opened by the Queen. And we could celebrate other signs of new life. The Anglican diocese of Southwark, where many parishes were full of problems far more difficult than those of the riverside area, was enabled to serve these disadvantaged and discouraged communities more effectively, and able and dedicated women were allowed to become priests.

When I knew the diocese it was still as problematic as when it had caused John Robinson to write *Honest to God*. Almost 2.5 million people lived in its 300 square miles. It offered about 400 churches to God and the people but the vast majority of the people seldom noticed. It included leafy suburbs but most of the boroughs closer to the cathedral were full of inner-city distress, and the estates of flats owned by local councils were full of personal depression. The social problems of this urban sprawl, repeated in other parts of England's once green and pleasant land, were analysed by a commission bravely appointed by Archbishop Runcie and a report was produced, *Faith in the City* (1985). One Conservative minister denounced it as 'Marxist theology' and others more legitimately complained that it had not costed its proposals, but the Church of England demonstrated its right to be taken seriously in this new manifestation of Christianity's traditional concern for the poor: it raised £45 million for new projects through the Church Urban Fund, often projects for much more use of church buildings by the communities around them. However, despite its title the report paid little attention to the problems of church life based on religious faith.

Back in the nineteenth century the bulk of the working class had largely lost contact with the churches, in the earlier years because the churches did not move to be with them from the countryside, and then because the 'mission churches', while useful as sources of 'charity' and having some appeal to women and children, were in no sense owned by working-class men. Then, in the twentieth century, the association of the churches with the respectability which women had supported was ended; the breakdown of family life was widespread; so was drug-related crime although of course many people remained quiet and decent. The very different culture of the middle classes was also largely alienated from the churches, but for very different reasons. In a relatively well-off area a church could belong, partly as a symbol of stable family life, partly because there could be a more explicitly religious response from the more reflective. But the real religion of the middle classes could not unfairly be said to concentrate on salaries, mortgages and supermarkets. These were the factors which had made South London something of a desert in terms of churchgoing.

So the placing of money as well as mouth alongside the deprived was a step full of promise, and in 1993, the year before my retirement, I was delighted that the cathedral where I served was the scene of the ordinations of the largest number of women priests to be ordained in any Anglican diocese anywhere. I knew that they would not be insensitive but would gently bring to the people desperately needed pastoral care and leadership. The pope had been prominent among those pleading with the Church of England not to take this step, and later the Vatican was to declare that his teaching on this matter belonged to the 'deposit of faith' (and was therefore infallible?), but when we feared that there would be demonstrations against the ordinations only one group appeared: some Roman Catholics were protesting against the delay in their own church. By 2002 women were about a fifth of the Church of England's full-time clergy and it seems possible that by the middle of the century they will outnumber the men.

*   *   *

That was the outcome of a debate lasting 20 years. In 1972 the Church of England's General Synod pondered a careful report which set out the arguments for and against. Three years later the majority felt ready to vote that 'there are no fundamental objections'. In 1984 the Bishop of Southwark presented our Diocesan Synod's request that women should be ordained and in the following year some were, but only as deacons. Then on 11 November 1992 the war of words came to an end, when the proposal to allow women to be priests was approved by two-thirds of the bishops, clergy and laity voting: two favourable votes in the House of Laity had supplied the majority needed. I had expected another disappointment but women had attracted more votes than the Methodists had done in the earlier test.

The Church could now at last receive leadership which women had previously been forbidden to contribute, ending an injustice to them and a great loss to the Church – and for several other reasons. One was that diversity had been recognized formally as an ingredient of unity. While those clergy who now decided to leave the Church of England (fewer than had been expected) went with a generous financial provision, parishes which did not want a woman to minister to them were also treated generously, even being allowed to have their own 'flying' (interdiocesan) bishops for sacramental purposes. I voted for these arrangements and am still convinced that they were right for the time being. Of course I do not think that they should be set in concrete as a permanent foundation for a denial of 'communion' within a church. Nor do I think that this minority's opposition ought to be allowed to prevent for much longer the logical sequel to women priests: women bishops.

After a long period when conservative minorities had been able to exercise a veto it had been recognized that the Church of England was entitled to obey its own majority's conscience even if it involved disagreements with the historic churches of Rome and the East and with 'Bible believers' in the West – but clearly my Church had not acted in a hurry, and the evidence provided by Scripture and Tradition had been urged on its anxious attention by its own members as well as by other counsellors. This particular disagreement had important precedents: the Church of England had rejected papal jurisdiction since the 1530s and in later controversies had rejected fundamentalism. Loyalty to the hope of reunion has always had to be balanced with loyalty to the truth, as all have agreed, but now the Church of England had made up its mind and the hope had to be that critics would sooner or later come to see a truth which Anglicans had themselves taken some time to admit. The official line, motivated by pastoral and ecumenical sensitivity, was that time was needed for a process of 'reception', which made it theoretically possible that the decision would be cancelled – but in reality the decision had been made irreversibly by those parts of the Anglican Communion which were ready for it.

It had been acknowledged that loyalty to the message of the Bible does not necessarily mean that parts of the Bible which belong to a vanished culture must be treated as permanently authoritative. One of the arguments in the controversy had been about whether women could be priests when the apostles had all been men; another whether women could 'represent Christ' at the altar; another whether by using the Greek word *kephalé* Paul had meant that Man was the 'source' or the 'head' of Woman in his first letter to Corinth (11.3). I now hoped that it would eventually be agreed that the apostles had themselves not been priests, since in the days of the New Testament no Christian was called a 'priest' except Christ; that as the mission of the apostles had been carried on by later generations, making a new idea of priesthood acceptable, women (while not priests) had usually represented Christ more effectively than had been found possible by men, especially men in senior positions; and that whether or not Paul, who assumed the historicity of Adam and Eve, also believed in the subordination of women to a male 'source' or 'head' was not decisive for Christians called to serve the mission now. Long before this controversy it had been seen that it was not necessary to believe that women should be forbidden to pray bareheaded (despite 1 Corinthians 11.13) or to teach men (despite

1 Timothy 2.12). Now I hoped that it would be acknowledged how revolutionary Jesus had been in his attitude to women – and how grateful Paul had been to all those leading women greeted by name at the end of his letter to Rome including Prisca his 'fellow-worker' (named before her husband) and Junia ('eminent among the apostles'). His first letter to Corinth mentioned a report to him by 'Chloe's people' (1.11). The arguments which came out of Rome in the 1990s, claiming that *The Ordination of Women in the Catholic Church* was unthinkable, were demolished in a book with that title in 2001 by John Wijngaards, a scholar who had resigned as a priest rather than accept the blanket of silence imposed by the Vatican.

*　　　*　　　*

When these women were ordained in 1993 (many of them had waited for many years) I saw more clearly the Church that could be, with many women in leadership, but I could not feel that the admission of women to the priesthood ought to be the end of the reconstruction of the Church and of the ordained ministry which serves Christ through the Church. The conviction has grown in me – as in many others – that the entire shape of the Church is wrong when it is imagined that a full-time minister, male or female, is required if the Word of God is to be preached, sacraments administered with proper authority and the pastoral work done.

That is not the picture given to us in the New Testament, where it is nowhere said who is to preside at the Eucharist but there is a rich variety of ministries: 'some to be apostles, some prophets, some evangelists, some pastors and teachers, to equip God's people for work in his service' (Ephesians 4.11, 12). In the little church in Corinth, which was full of scandals discussed frankly by Paul in his first letter, there were gifts from the 'Spirit of God' of wise or profound speech, of faith or powers of healing, of miracle-working, of prophecy or discernment, of speaking in 'tongues' of ecstasy (*glossolalia*) or the ability to interpret, and of love which is the most important gift of all (12.4; 13.13). It seems to follow that in many congregations in our own time there are spiritual gifts waiting to be unlocked. Some gifts are given to the old who can contribute not only time (the privilege of the retired) but also the calm wisdom which can come from experience of life; presumably the 'elders' who minister in the churches in the New Testament were not all young. Other gifts are, however, given to people, usually young themselves, who do not feel strangers in the youth culture. There ought to be 'evangelists' who have a gift for communicating the Gospel in conversation – and 'deacons' whose gift is to communicate it by loving service which is practical. All these gifts can be acknowledged by a formal commissioning, although that is not a necessity. And among these gifts is likely to be the ability to preside at the Eucharist, which requires no long training but does require authorization, which means ordination, by the church concerned. The 'lay presidency' advocated by some Evangelicals would greatly damage the cause of Christian unity, but an orderly arrangement could mean a full and frequent Eucharist in almost every church in the country. That would greatly strengthen church life in the villages – and in the towns it would bring back what worked well in the days of the New Testament. Many suggestions and experiments have been made along these lines but not nearly enough has been done.

Such a development need not in any way detract from the importance of teaching, emphasized in the New Testament far more than the presidency of the Eucharist. The paid clergy could be encouraged to concentrate on teaching, and could be joined by many who already exercise this gift in universities, colleges and schools. Others could be equipped to use modern methods of educating adults and children, perhaps involving for adults the use of videos followed by discussion, and for children activity rather than formal instruction: music-making, for example, or appropriate conversation. The traditional sermon is too long for what is now the normal span of attention and in most churches it would be far more useful to interject short statements or commentaries into the flow of liturgical words, music and actions. For this, not much academic training is needed but it does depend on the personality: if that communicates, people will listen. And short statements which are worth hearing may take hours to prepare.

Nor should such developments in life and learning within the congregation detract from the importance of 'house churches' or 'cells' which meet in people's homes. Such groups are strongly linked with New Testament days and have been vital in some of the most exciting growth in the Church of our own time – in the basic communities which brought Latin American Catholicism into the midst of the poor, for example, or in the spread of Christianity in East Asia. They are not a panacea: in some situations the idea of a meeting in a home may seem very strange, in some the 'cell' may become absorbed in its own small self, in some it may be cut off from fellow Christians by favouring a do-it-yourself religion, in some it may be dominated and manipulated by its leader. But these are dangers, not the necessary consequences of a strategy for spiritual and numerical growth which includes fellowships more intimate than a congregation's.

*   *   *

It does not seem unthinkable that the hopes of the 1960s for the churches' renewal including a much larger measure of unity can be revived in a new century, having acquired more realism, and the 2001 report on Anglican/Methodist relations could turn out to have been a new beginning despite its caution. Names matter less than realities, yet getting a name right can be a good first step in establishing an authentic relationship between people or institutions. Being told the right name can also be a help to people who are invited to add themselves to such a relationship. It may therefore be useful to submit a suggestion that the main churches in Britain could be renamed in the near future. Although this is probably a suggestion as unrealistic as the 1980 date for reunion, they could be called the Church 'in England', 'in Scotland' or 'in Wales', adding in brackets (Anglican), (Roman Catholic), (Presbyterian), (Methodist), etc. This change would not automatically affect the right of all the churches to retain their own doctrines and self-understanding: without pretending to be the 'Church of England' or the 'Church of Scotland' a church with a great tradition could continue to aim at a nationwide mission and ministry (as does what is now the Anglican 'Church in Wales'), 'the Roman Catholic Church in England and Wales' could continue to teach that the Body of Christ most clearly 'subsists in' Christians in communion with the pope, and Methodists (etc.) could continue to honour their own origins and international connections. Any local church which was not willing to make the change when it had been explained and discussed should not be compelled. Also, a short Act of Parliament could ensure that the use of the new name would not affect the legal position of any church.

The use of this name, while of course not essential, could be a purposeful symbol that the participating churches fully accept what they have already declared to be the truth: that the churches now sharing a name already share membership of the Church of Christ through baptism and through a common 'confession' of the 'apostolic' or 'essential' faith. If any invited church drew back from this definite and public step, that refusal could be noted as a question mark to be set against its declared commitment to the ecumenical movement. And the new name displayed outside the church building could be a signal to the public that inside the building was a vision, a prayer and a hope. Certainly to informed Christians, and hopefully to a wider circle, the new name could be matched with the New Testament's language about the Church 'in Jerusalem', 'in Ephesus' or 'in Corinth'.

The new name – or any other big move to make the churches keep in step – would not necessarily involve any official authorization of the practice of sharing Holy Communion together. Nor would it automatically bring any official recognition that all the ministers in the participating churches 'administer' the Word and Sacraments without any defect. Since the churches would retain their own identities joint acts of worship would be rare in comparison with worship according to their own traditions, and no doubt some of their members would feel it wrong for them to take part in joint eucharistic worship. But it seems probable that if these churches could more thoroughly acknowledge each other as belonging to the Church of Christ, a fuller recognition of the Word as preached in them, and of the sacraments as celebrated in them, would be widely thought to follow in logic as well as in charity. It has already come to pass in agreements between Anglicans and Lutherans. And any conscientious difficulty could be eased or ended if without further delay all the participating churches could have bishops ordained by existing bishops in the historic succession, as a sign of unity with the universal ('Catholic') Church in all places and all ages.

It does seem still possible to hope that the experience of spiritual communion between the churches, which has already produced an unprecedented degree of mutual recognition and respect, will in due course lead to a desire for a fuller and more formal reconciliation. Clearly this must involve acts in which the participating churches explicitly pray for the Holy Spirit to bestow whatever is needed for an enlarged ministry. If this is genuinely meant as prayer, it ought to be agreed that God need not be informed about precisely what is needed on the basis of sound theology clearly explained to him. It would be in keeping with the New Testament's repeated insistence on humility if the existing bishops were to be the first to ask for this prayer to be said over them and given the traditional – not magical –

expression of the 'laying of hands'. (In their Appeal to All Christian People for Christian unity the Anglican bishops in the Lambeth Conference of 1920 declared their willingness to take part in such an act.) Prayer by bishops and others over the ministers of all the participating churches could follow this act, not implying that any earlier ministry had been invalid, but clearly authorizing all to minister everywhere when invited.

It would be a betrayal of the vision of the kingdom of God were ecumenical progress to be confined to new words and acts regarding the mutual acknowledgement and reconciliation of churches which would in practice remain largely separate. If the public is to believe that Christians really love each other and their neighbours, practical co-operation must grow on a scale not yet seen and I still see no reason to alter the principle stated in 1952, that churches should 'act together on all matters except those in which deep divisions of conviction compel them to act separately'. Such co-operation would surely result in a much larger, much deeper and much more effective desire for the churches' visible reunion. That is the goal which the whole ecumenical movement shares in theory – but which is now usually placed in the unimaginable future. From the New Testament the question arises: why are we waiting?

*   *   *

Is it possible that the largest of all the churches could one day take part in such a reunion on terms acceptable both to itself and to Orthodox, Protestant and Anglican churches?

As I write, it seems impossible – and it may be right for an Anglican to sum up the reasons, since Catholicism looking to Rome is the church from which Anglicanism came and to which it ought to be delighted to return. Despite the changes which flowed from the Second Vatican Council, and despite the hopes still held by a multitude of Roman Catholics who regard themselves as being loyal to the spirit which predominated at the council, the dismissal of the married laity's consciences, wishes and advice about birth control by Paul VI in 1968 has been followed by a tightening of thought control over the clergy, including theologians, during the long reign of John Paul II. Both popes deserve the gratitude of all Christians as being great spiritual leaders who said many wise things and did many brave things, but the overall effect has been to strengthen the impressions that the papacy is the world's last monarchy with absolute power and that an international church, over all of which a pope has jurisdiction in theory and in practice, is officially bound to follow papal policy in general and in detail. It makes reunion with any church not willing to accept such dictatorship impossible.

In 2002 I see no prospect of a quick change. The official self-understanding of the Roman Catholic Church is that it was promised infallibility by Christ, although all the surviving evidence points against the church in Rome having a 'bishop' in our sense of the word before AD 140. This freedom from error is said to be enjoyed by the present Bishop of Rome 'when he proclaims by a definitive act a doctrine pertaining to faith and morals', and such definitions of doctrine are 'irreformable of themselves and not from the consent of the Church'. Infallibility is also present when the body of bishops proposes for belief a doctrine to which the pope agrees. It covers what has been 'divinely revealed', especially in the teaching of Christ, but decisions about what has been revealed belong to the pope and the bishops, and in practice infallibility has been claimed for doctrines which are not explicit in Scripture. Even when infallibility is not claimed for teaching about faith and morals, if such teaching 'leads to a better understanding of revelation' (as decided by the pope and the bishops), the faithful are obliged to 'adhere with a religious assent' and are legally liable to be 'disciplined' if they do not.

Hans Küng's short history of *The Catholic Church* (2001) was not so short that it could not include a representative selection of the errors which have been made on this basis across the centuries – and in many bigger books he has set out his reasons for thinking them errors and for offering alternatives. Some errors made in the past have been admitted by recent popes, and by the Second Vatican Council, either explicitly or by implication. However, it has never been declared officially that, being human, the Church must always be capable of error, even at the highest level and even when a bishops' council deliberates. In practice the decisive facts are that the Second Vatican Council left the papacy with unrestricted power; the pope now appoints almost all the bishops in the Roman Catholic Church; the bishops allocate priests to parishes; and the bishops and priests are not obliged to take advice from the laity on any matter at all. (Thus a parish priest can simply abolish a parish council.) Despite all the activity of the Holy Spirit, humanity cannot escape error and corruption when given power on that scale. Tragically, the old Orthodox, Protestant and Anglican objection that the Church of Rome has erred has not yet lost all its force.

But there is the hope that the leaders of this church may in due course revise their teaching about their own authority by reflecting more deeply about the Church's duty to be a model to society, a model pointing to the kingdom of God. In a radical departure from the past, the Second Vatican Council taught that 'nobody may be forced to act against his convictions, nor is anyone to be restrained from acting in accord with his conscience in religious matters' – not even if a dissenter fails to live up to the obligation of 'seeking the truth and adhering to it'. And in its social teaching this church – which used to support authoritarian regimes, like the Church of England – thus defines the 'subsidiarity' which it recommends: 'a community of a higher order should not interfere with the internal life of a community of a lower order, depriving it of its functions, but rather should support it in case of need and help to co-ordinate its activity with the activities of the rest of society, always with a view to the common good'.

Despite active discouragement from the Vatican, there has already been much discussion between Catholics about the application of these principles to church life: a good collection of essays, with a bibliography, is *Governance and Authority in the Roman Catholic Church* edited by Noel Timms and Kenneth Wilson (2000). Many of the reforms suggested must seem, at least to onlookers, obviously right for pastoral reasons. In teaching about sexual activity the consciences of the married and of homosexuals ought to be respected, if not by approval then by a halt to denunciations. Marriage ought to be allowed to all priests who do not have a vocation to celibacy, as it already is in the Eastern Catholic churches and for ex-Anglicans. These reforms would do much to restore the credibility of the clergy, severely shaken if not destroyed by many recent scandals involving the sexual abuse of boys or hidden sexual relationships with women. In most areas of the world, traditional or modern, the total renunciation of sexual activity seems so contrary to nature that it does not automatically earn respect, but the sexual exploitation of vulnerable women or young people by the clergy does automatically earn disgust and contempt. If the authorities of the Roman Catholic Church could fully come to terms with these facts – a process which has begun – they could expect to see more of the laity consulting their priests about moral problems, although it would also seem wise to encourage the rise of corporate services of repentance and reconciliation as an alternative to the private confession of sins. (Neither the celibacy of priests nor private confession to them was the practice in the early centuries of the Church.)

The end of the insistence on celibacy could also be expected to help in the recruitment of priests. In many (not all) parts of the Roman Catholic Church the shortage of priests is the biggest practical problem for bishops; it is estimated that in Europe about half the parishes have no resident priest and that in Latin America as a whole, 8,000 Catholics are served, or not served, by one priest. To exalt the rule about celibacy over the need to make the sacraments available to the laity can seem to be a severe error in any bishop's faith. The Catholic laity would have to support the families of full-time clergy, but so do the laity of all other churches already.

The principle of subsidiarity, preached by bishops to governments, ought to be applied to the Church. It ought to involve regular councils to which all bishops would be invited (say, twice in a century); more frequent meetings of some senior diocesan bishops to join the pope in the supervision of the Vatican's bureaucracy; more powers put clearly in the hands of bishops' conferences of nations or continents; and local elections of bishops after careful consultations with the clergy and laity of the diocese concerned. It would also ensure the creation and permanence of councils representing the laity and exercising responsibility and real influence in Rome and in every diocese and parish. Conferences are less important than such constitutional changes, but the situations ought to be reformed which have resulted in no World Congress for the Lay Apostolate being held in Rome since 1967 and no National Pastoral Congress being held in Britain since 1980.

Subsidiarity is particularly important in connection with the need for 'inculturation', often discussed but inadequately practised because often not permitted by the Vatican. In Latin America the hopes raised by the spread of the 'base communities' of the laity, and by 'liberation' theology, have been dashed by many appointments of unsympathetic bishops. In Africa and Asia the bold adaptation of European Catholic practices to local traditions of worship and spirituality has often been discouraged or vetoed by the Vatican, despite some theoretical approval. In Europe protests against the Vatican's lack of understanding have been made not only by theologians but also by millions signing petitions with the slogan 'We are the

Church'. The situation often seems as explosive as it was in the age of Luther – but now there is no need to found a Protestant church: an easier answer is to withdraw from churchgoing, or at any rate from active contacts with the clergy.

It has been said that the division into two Catholic Churches which was evident before the Second Vatican Council – between the ordained church with a duty to teach and the baptized church with a duty to believe and obey – has been replaced by a division into a traditionalist church, mainly clerical, and a progressive church, mainly lay. In some situations, however, that generalization can be reversed: there the clergy 'cry forward' and the laity 'cry back'. The suggestions which I have outlined would be designed to reduce the tensions not by destroying traditions about the essentials but by making reforms which would strengthen the Church in its service to the kingdom of God in the modern world.

In 2002 a reforming Third Vatican Council cannot be expected with any confidence, but the Second was totally unexpected before John XXIII announced that he felt inspired to summon it – and with or without a new council there may be a new reformation, breaking to the surface like water which has been underground. In the sixteenth century reformation, Protestant or Catholic, was not expected: the medieval Church looked secure, many attempts to reform it 'in head and members' had achieved little, the storm which overwhelmed the system of 1,000 years was sudden. The scientist Stephen Jay Gould has described evolution as 'punctuated equilibrium' because it develops by sudden spurts after long periods of stability. The same two words will do as a summary of the history of the Christian Church – and looking back, it can seem that time after time the equilibrium was punctured by the God of surprises who, far from being an inactive spectator, is powerfully involved in what he loves. So are we in the midst of a new and better re-formation?

CHAPTER 6

Evangelical and True

THE VITALITY OF THE Evangelical movement since the Second World War has made me think long and hard. Despite claims, it has not replaced Catholicism in areas where that church is 'the usual one' and it has not converted the millions needed to recall a predominantly secular society back into regular churchgoing – but the fact is that its growth has been spectacular in both the Americas and substantial in many other places including Britain. It has been specially impressive in two ways. It has revived the centrality of the Bible in Christian teaching, worship and prayer, drawing on a unique and inexhaustible spiritual reservoir – once again, for many earlier creative movements in the history of Christianity have had the same inspiration. And it has revived the impact of the Bible's central message on human lives. The most obvious impact has been emotional: deep feelings have been stirred by the arousal of a sense that life has become meaningless if not positively evil, and then by the admission of God into one's own life, sometimes with excitement, often with transforming practical consequences, and then by a growing relationship with Jesus Christ as one's personal Master and Saviour, Friend and Lord. An enthusiasm without inhibitions has been the most striking phenomenon of this revival of personal religion. It can attract the poor whose normal life is anything but exciting, but it can also appeal to people with more money than meaning in their lives. Like the 'religion of the heart' in the eighteenth and nineteenth centuries, this revival has pumped new blood into Christianity.

All this has struck me because I have been heavily involved in the Student Christian Movement which has had a very different character. In 1960 I wrote a short history of the SCM and called it *Movements into Tomorrow*. At that stage about 8,000 students belonged to its branches or to theological colleges affiliated to it and I saw no reason why, as student numbers grew, the work could not grow too, persuading the intelligent, teaching tomorrow's teachers and preaching sensibly to tomorrow's sensible preachers. But what grew was an Evangelical movement, the Universities and Colleges Christian Fellowship, now with about 15,000 students meeting for Bible study each week, with enthusiastic branches and conferences, with support from many scholars, with an annual budget of more than £1.5 million, and with a 'doctrinal basis' unchanged since the 1920s. But although many chaplains to students do work which is like what it used to do, the SCM itself has dwindled. Although its full-time co-ordinators, numbering three, are now in touch with about 60 groups affiliated to it, many of these groups are not called 'SCM'. Although confidence in SCM work has recently been shown by the raising of an endowment fund, expenditure has been restricted by an annual income of about £75,000. I have learned by the hard way to salute the Evangelicals' success.

*   *   *

The SCM was born out of the Evangelical revival of the 1870s, when many students began to offer themselves for lifelong service as missionaries overseas. In the 1890s the extraordinarily confident 'watchword' emerged: 'the evangelization of the world in this generation'. So did the SCM, a national body combining branches which were usually called Christian Unions. But with an input from teachers such as the young William Temple, long before he became an archbishop, the SCM developed quite a sophisticated interest first in social and then in intellectual questions, for these were found to be important both in the countries to which evangelists went and in the Europe to which war came. Students were still influenced by the SCM to become missionaries overseas but in 1910 the Cambridge Inter-Collegiate Christian Union, which had preserved a simple form of Evangelical 'Bible believing' since the beginning of the daily prayer meeting in 1862, decided that it could no longer be affiliated to the more broadly based SCM. When its representatives asked the leaders of the national movement whether they put the 'atoning blood' of Christ at the centre of their message, they got a response which did not satisfy. It was not that the SCM ignored the cross: in the Aim and Basis which it adopted in 1919 it declared that 'it is only when we see on Calvary the price of suffering paid day by day by God himself for all human sin that we can enter into the experience of true penitence and forgiveness, which sets us free to embark on a wholly new way of life'. That phraseology was influenced by the mood of the time: divine suffering was widely believed in for the first time as a result of the Great War but the new League of Nations was a symbol of hope for a new world. However, it was surely wrong to claim that this is the only meaning of the cross. By insisting on this basis the SCM lost contact with Christian students who maintained an older theology and whose successors formed the Inter-Varsity Fellowship of Evangelical Unions in 1928.

To many the IVF seemed narrow in comparison with the SCM, which by 1935 had 11,500 members out of a total student population of 72,000. This broader movement played a leading role in the life of many of the churches, especially in the ecumenical movement. It also provided an education in national and international affairs and the Second World War made it less optimistically 'liberal', influenced now by the 'neo-orthodoxy' of Karl Barth in a return to the Bible and by the 'Christian realism' of Reinhold Niebuhr with its emphasis on a fallen humanity's selfishness, tragedy and catastrophic sin. But in the 1960s optimism returned – and, with it, a depth of participation in the progressive causes of the day but a shallowness in religion.

In 1965 I was asked to serve for a year as general secretary of the movement while remaining the publisher at the SCM Press. I tried to begin a project of extending the work on a reduced budget by stressing student leadership and by making the SCM more of an agency serving the denominational chaplaincies which had multiplied on the scene but were inevitably local in any outreach. For the first time a Roman Catholic priest was appointed to the staff. The intention was to stimulate studies which would wrestle both with the Bible and with contemporary realities. My hopes were high but foolish. As the 1960s progressed support from the SCM's senior friends and from the churches decreased drastically and as the movement went further and further to the theological and political Left the student membership also plunged. Most students now had no background in the churches but could be enthusiastic about particular good causes. They could be willing to argue about big issues, preferably over a drink, but not to go to a meeting of an organization which could be mocked as the Slightly Christian Movement.

There were special factors in Britain and Ireland but essentially the story was repeated in other countries, as was recorded in Risto Lehtonen's *Story of a Storm* (1998).

In contrast, the firmly Evangelical student movement largely overcame its internal problems and its story was celebrated in Geraint Fielder's *Lord of the Years* (1988). The ethos had been middle class, with initiatives from the 'varsities' of Oxbridge and fond memories of evangelistic camps for public schoolboys. Many of the big names had excelled in gentlemanly sports. Although the Inter-Varsity Fellowship had been suspicious of the 'academic approach' to religion its own preferred method had been teaching through a sermon or lecture without a discussion. Its devotional life had been fed by a close study of the words of the written Word of God and its morality had been strict, in the Puritan tradition. Now the Christian Unions faced a student world in which even the most gracious *machismo* or snobbery was completely out of place. Students, female or male, poor or posh, became anxious about debts, degrees and jobs, and while they tried to keep up with the lectures, wanted to relax in such leisure as they had. Brought up on TV, and later on computers, they preferred images and soundbites to pages of reading, so that if a religious happening were to be attractive it would probably have to be a 'celebration'. For the 'religious' minority the charismatic movement's almost Pentecostal concentration on personal experience of the Holy Spirit's often dramatic power could be an alternative to humble dependence on the printed Bible. From another angle, the old authority of Scripture could be made more complicated, for Evangelicals were now to be found among the scholars who accepted what had once seemed shocking, 'criticism' of the Bible on historical or literary grounds. And Evangelicals were now to be found among those who answered ethical questions by asking what was true love in a given situation. But many students have liked what they have found in the Christian Unions: a clear offer of a happier, more purposeful life in a strong fellowship which can become a second family, with a network of friendly support continuing after student days. Thus many reasons can be given for the success of this strongly Evangelical movement, but in my view the supreme reasons have been that it kept assets which the SCM largely lost in the 1960s: fascinations with the Bible and with Christ.

Having faced the fact that the SCM is unlikely to be revived on its former scale, I have asked myself what could be the future of the organized Christian presence in the British universities and colleges.

The question matters because it is intended that half of the population will experience higher education, often deciding their adult identities in this environment. Will the Evangelical witness to Christ be such that more and more young people will recognize in it a passion for truth and a grappling with reality? Will that, plus the pastoral work of chaplains, be enough? Or will the churches have to admit that they will be disastrously defeated in this strategic area unless they directly and with energetic urgency sponsor more activities as introductions to an adult Christianity? It would not seem too difficult for the churches to organize regional or national conferences for students, recruiting mainly through the chaplains accredited by the different churches but hopefully ecumenical, since one of the urgent needs is that more young people should have experiences which make them think more seriously about ecumenical hopes and problems. Already many students have glimpsed a more ecumenical future through conferences in Britain under mainly Evangelical sponsorship (such as Greenbelt) or through visits to the French ecumenical community which has been a magnet to young people in Taizé. The need is for conferences not taking any commitment for granted, with students as prominent as possible and with minimal expenses, but the churches' best voices ought to be heard, even if only to be contradicted. One activity could be a discussion of a video raising controversial issues, in order to demonstrate what Christian discernment is and is not. Worship could be experimental. Grants might be secured from charities which exist in order to encourage religious education. If the feeling in the churches is that no resources are available to support such a project, the reply must be made that wise farmers do not refuse to buy seed.

*   *   *

It is very encouraging that many Evangelical teachers have been ready to listen to criticism. Whether or not they have been willing to be called postconservative, they have certainly been courageous and constructive. While not abandoning what they see as essentials, they have moved away from the tendency of many of their predecessors to understand Evangelicalism as a systematic opposition to modernity which, however, mirrors modernity in some vitally important ways: so far as it can, it defends the Bible as accurate scientifically and historically and it defends theology as a consistently rational deduction from the evidence which is clearly set out in 'God's Word written'. That old simplicity is impossible for the new teachers. Instead they have frankly acknowledged that Evangelicals in good standing take different positions on a large range of topics.

Some current differences go back to controversies which meant that in the age of the Reformation there could be no Protestant united front. Luther and Calvin were divided from Zwingli in understanding the Lord's Supper, for which Luther kept the old name 'Mass'. Luther, Calvin and Zwingli were all divided from the Anabaptists in answering the question whether baptism should be confined to adult believers. Arminius and the Wesleys were divided from Calvin over the question whether Christ died in order to save all or only those predestined to salvation. Protestants have preferred different ways of worship, different forms of church government and different relationships with the state. They have disagreed over whether only the ordained should preside at the Lord's Supper and whether only those who can testify to a decisive crisis should be counted among the converted. Some have owned slaves; others have freed slaves.

Fresh differences between Evangelicals became noticeable in the twentieth century. Their temperament is not the same in Latin as in North America, in Europe as in Africa, in India as in China. Are Evangelicals pacifists? Are they racists? Do they expect God's blessing to be followed by prosperity or by suffering? In modern politics they are on the Right or on the Left. They can differ about questions of morality. Do they drink alcohol or go to dances or cinemas? Is marriage after divorce ever right? Is sex before marriage always gravely sinful? They can also differ about new doctrinal questions. Must traditional views about the Bible's composition, authorship and authority be accepted nowadays? How accurate is the history in the Bible? Are some of the stories of miracles not to be taken literally? What about the second coming of Christ? Is heaven possible only for Christians who die trusting in Christ alone? Is hell a 'place' of everlasting punishment, or do people who finally reject God simply lose their lives?

Moreover, the twentieth century brought urgent questions about church life, answered differently by different Evangelicals. Is it right for women to be speakers and leaders in churches? What is the 'headship' of men now? Is the Bible itself open to criticism as being patriarchal? Should 'shepherding' by pastors be dominant or gentle? How readily should 'discipline' be used? Should preaching concentrate on the calm exposition of a text, or on the passionate communication of an experience? Should all Christians follow the example of the Pentecostal churches (which are divided) with their ecstatic speaking in 'tongues', prophecies voiced by members of the congregation, and miraculous healings including the acknowledge- ment and expulsion of demons? Should Evangelicals be active members of churches which are not fully Evangelical? Or should they gather in a church which is clearly faithful according to their faith? Or should they concentrate on support for 'parachurch' movements dedicated to evangelism or charitable work? And should they co-operate with any willing Christians?

Recently a disagreement between Evangelicals has begun to appear about the method by which such questions should be answered. In the postmodern mood which began about 1950 there was a change of emphasis, seeing that being reasonable may include taking account of emotions, intuitions and visions; that being pro- gressive may include coming to terms with many realities which are complicated; and that being knowledgeable may mean being wise rather than accurate. It may therefore be thought reasonable to make progress by being made wise through stories and symbols, rather than by knock-down commands or proofs – or by strip-down history claimed to be free of all mythology. This new approach can be associated with postmodernism, yet it is also something of a revival of the attitude of the ancient world to the writing of religious or other literature, which originated in stories told around a fire in the evening.

This more subtle understanding of what being 'true' means is being advocated in respected Evangelical circles, especially by teach- ers who communicate with the rising generation. In Britain several such voices have been raised, perhaps most influentially in the Bible Society's project to encourage reflection about 'hermeneutics' (but it is a pity that the encouragement of a meaningful interpretation of the Bible should be called by a name understood only by the elite). The discussion in North America has been much more extensive and intense: it was well summed up by Stanley Grenz in *Renewing the Center* (2000), ending with his own well-argued plea for an 'ortho- doxy' which would be 'celebrative' but also 'generous' and therefore 'hopeful'. These Evangelical explorers do not defend postmodernism as defined by Jean-François Lyotard, 'incredulity towards meta- narratives', for to them the story told in the Christian Bible is still

supreme above all other stories. But they are Christian postmod-
ernists in the sense that they agree in thinking that the Word given by
God has been given more in stories than in statements, more in
people than in propositions, more in symbols than in formulations,
and more in visions than in laws – with everything expressed in the
language of a particular time and place in order that it may be translated by us into our lives under the guidance of the Spirit of the
living God. 'The ultimate authority in the Church', says Grenz, 'is
the Spirit speaking through Scripture.'

This new stirring in American Evangelical thought contradicts the
widely held belief that American Evangelicals in general do not
think. Only some of the many millions of Americans who now identify themselves as born-again Christians are fundamentalists in the
strict style of the 1920s, when 'Bible believing' was mixed up with a
general attitude of backwoods reaction – but many other large
groups, inside as well as outside the USA and inside as well as
outside Christianity, can still find in this tradition plenty to dislike.
Catholics can protest that Evangelical spirituality is narrow and
shallow in comparison with a heritage which encircles the globe and
goes deep into the history of the saints. The Eastern Orthodox can
despise this novelty, deter its missionaries and take pride in their
own tradition of dignified worship and self-denying holiness ready
for martyrdom. Churches which look neither to Rome nor to Byzan-
tium but to Luther or Calvin can think that this cult of happy
success is unimpressive in comparison with their own sober religion
based on solid theology and some willingness to suffer. And other
groups can find here nothing at all to admire, because these loud-
mouthed Americans appear to think themselves superior not only to
modern knowledge but also to the older world with its varied faiths
and moralities. And perhaps the basic factor is that much of the contemporary world is bitterly anti-American, even while it wants
American products, so that it sees American religion as spread
alongside neocolonialism and as embodied in TV evangelists who
most enjoy reading 'In God We Trust' when it is printed on dollar
bills sent to them by the gullible.

This prejudice or verdict has not been entirely ended by the
spread of Pentecostalism. This can confirm the worst fears because it
seems to treat as the climax of its evangelism an ecstatic 'speaking in
tongues' which abandons every trace of rationality.

The phenomenon is undeniably genuine and meets human needs –

not only in societies with a deeply rooted belief in the power of many spirits often unholy by Christian standards. Even in societies where this is not the Christian believer's environment the experience can be a liberation from formality and boredom – and at a deeper level from dependence on someone else's claim to be the divine Spirit's mouthpiece. A volcano-like eruption can release emotions previously suppressed in obedience to a social or religious code of respectability, or concealed because it is wise to hide emotions when one is employed to perform mechanical tasks (either as a peasant or, with much more pay, in front of a computer). This explains why the Pentecostal movement has grown so widely from its origins in the USA and why other churches have recently included many of its characteristics. But the criticism of Pentecostalism becomes not prejudice but a sustainable Christian protest when the ecstasy which can be rationalized as hysteria is regarded as the necessary ticket of entry into Christian life in the first class. It is true that in the Acts of the Apostles a first-class story-teller begins the history of the Christian mission to the world with the picturesque drama of a 'strong, driving wind' and 'flames' and with the miracle of immediate speech in many 'tongues' meaning ordinary languages. It is also true that the later gift of the Holy Spirit to Samaritans and Gentiles was, Luke says, so dramatic that it could impress a magician (Acts 8.18) and reduce hesitant Jews to silence (Acts 11.5–18). And in his first letter to Corinth (chapter 14) Paul could be thankful that he was 'more gifted in tongues than any of you'. Yet he could say that his exercise of this gift would be useless unless he could teach in plain language, understood by his hearers, for otherwise his speech would be 'gibberish' and a congregation all speaking like this would seem 'mad' to any unbeliever who might be present. To Paul, 'speaking in tongues' is 'talking with God' and therefore 'may build up the speaker himself', but thousands of such words are less desirable than five which are intelligible – and are 'nothing' in comparison with love.

Many American Evangelical thinkers now active and influential are not to be condemned on any of these grounds, however. Certainly they are not fundamentalists adhering to the 'old-time religion' as the centre of an anti-modern package. Nor are their loyalties closed to any other movement, ancient or modern, which deserves courteous, thoughtful and constructive dialogue. And the preachers and professors who are leading Evangelicals into this more open mindset (not into embracing every passing fad) consistently use reasoning language, whether or not they also approve of the 'speaking in tongues' which Paul told the Corinthians not to forbid. It therefore seems realistic to hope that Evangelicals everywhere, who have always been heavily influenced by developments in the USA, will gradually move in the same direction.

*   *   *

John Stott has been called by Billy Graham 'the most respected Evangelical clergyman in the world today' and he deserves all the other praise gathered in the two-volume biography of him by Timothy Dudley-Smith. Perhaps impertinently I asked him to allow me to offer an appreciation and criticism of his many writings, to which he would reply. He accepted and our friendly dialogue was published under the title *Essentials* (in the American and Chinese editions *Evangelical Essentials*). I did not then reply to his replies but I now offer some reflections, helped by his *Evangelical Truth* (1999).

What I asked him to reconsider was the insistence on certain words. Two of these are about the authority of the Bible, stated in many declarations of Evangelical faith since the 1820s to be 'infallible' or 'inerrant'. The *Oxford English Dictionary* gives as the meaning of the first word 'not liable to be deceived or mistaken' and as the meaning of the second 'does not err'. Because he feels uncomfortable with such negatives, Dr Stott has preferred to say with another Evangelical leader, James Packer, that 'Evangelicals are essentially concerned to defend the Bible's total trustworthiness as a consequence of entire truthfulness', and in 1999 he was willing to be one of those who use the simple phrase 'what the Bible says, God says'. But being well aware of modern 'critical' scholarship, he has often qualified that simplicity by teaching that Scripture is authoritative '(a) as originally given and (b) as correctly interpreted' and that the correct interpretation must be based on what 'the Bible affirms' when 'taken as a whole'. This seems to leave room for questions about particular reports or commands in Scripture.

My dialogue with him has left me still asking whether these qualifications are enough to counteract a style in the use of the Bible in the churches – not only by Evangelicals – which may easily suggest that it is indeed believed that the Bible is without error, a belief which is plainly contrary to the facts. The phrase 'The word of the Lord', or 'This is the word of the Lord', is now often used after a public reading from the Bible. In most cases this is right – but not always. The desire to be conservatively ecumenical, which is one of the motives here, is also right – but not always.

Unless God dictated the Christians' Bible into human minds which were the ancient equivalent of modern recording machines – a theory rejected by Dr Stott and many other Evangelical teachers in recent years – there is no way in which all the events and speech contained in it can have been reproduced with machine-like reliability. That applies not only to conversations which took place in private but also to the words spoken by Jesus in public, as is shown by the variations between the gospels and in the material taken by Matthew and Luke from their common source. And although memories were no doubt often better before they were bombarded by the modern input of information and entertainment, it is also clear that before modern styles of research and writing developed, to be an historian did not mean always trying to be accurate. Luke, for example, opens his gospel by assuring the reader that he has 'investigated the whole course of these events in detail' and has decided to write an 'orderly narrative' – but immediately recounts a conversation between an angel and a priest more than 70 years previously.

The men who wrote the Bible did not take scrupulous care to consult and endorse what had been written previously, and those who collected *ta biblia* ('the books') to be 'canonical' (ruling faith) did not exclude writings which were very different from others. To take the Hebrew Bible: it begins with two creation myths which come from different traditions and it goes on with a great variety in style and substance. The 'Law of Moses' is not a single law: it can be shown to be a collection of legal traditions and some of its contents seem to have been collected some 800 years after the exodus from Egypt. The history of Israel is not a single chronicle. It is a collection of narratives also told in different periods; some are compatible with archaeology but others are not (for example, the evidence suggests that the conquest of Canaan was not so rapid or so bloody as it became in patriotic stories). When I wrote an introductory book called *A Key to the Old Testament* (new edition 1989) the key idea was that the Hebrew Bible is a library in which some of the rooms may need to be unlocked by an appreciation which is 'critical' – and from this library there are several exits, one of them Christian.

Like Jacob in one of the most instructive of their old tales, these people could believe that they had come across a bit of God after wrestling with a mysterious messenger from him – but in another story Moses was allowed to see no more than God's back. The people who wrote or recited the hymnal of the Jerusalem temple (our psalms) did so in a variety of needs, from joyous thanksgiving to the blackness of almost complete despair: God seemed sometimes very near and sometimes appallingly distant. Prophets proclaimed that they saw God at work not only in the history of Israel but also in the victories of the armies of Assyria and Babylon, savagely punishing the Israelites for their follies in provoking such empires and for their crippling divisions into two kingdoms and into rich and poor. Other prophets sustained their people in exile and had visions of glory as the exile ended. More calmly the sages on record in the 'wisdom' literature saw the Creator's work in the beauty and orderliness of the creation, including the relentless punishment of stupidity by disaster. In the end even Job saw God through his tears, lifting his eyes from his self-pitying laments to be overwhelmed by the majesty of the Creator in the astounding creation. Even the weary cynic who wrote the book called Ecclesiastes clung to the belief that, like the sun, God is there, looking down on the lives of fools and not often bringing them to an abrupt end. Taken together, these words wrung out of experience add up to a uniquely powerful statement of the unique importance of the wrestle with God. A superb exposition may be found in Walter Brueggemann's *Theology of the Old Testament*, his summary of a lifetime's work in 1997. But what is not clear is why any one sound coming out of all this wrestling should be regarded as 'infallible' or 'inerrant' or even as 'true'. It is too real, being a human cry to God in a human crisis, and if we want to hear the truth we have to hear all the cries.

All this is material which has to do with the history of a people and it seems reasonable to think of it as encouraging thought and action about the birth, freedom and growth of every people in the world. Indeed, some 750 years before Christ Amos taught that the same God brought Israel up from Egypt and the hated Philistines from Caphtor (9.7), and when the Israelites were being crushed by these empires Isaiah seemed to hear Yahweh the God of Israel calling Egypt 'my people' and Assyria 'my handiwork' (19.25). The novel which is the story of Jonah ends up in God's compassion for Nineveh the capital of Assyria and the novel which is the story of Ruth tells how an Arab girl came to Bethlehem and thus to the family tree of King David. But as almost everyone has agreed, it does not seem reasonable to believe that all later generations are closely bound to the stories and laws of Ancient Israel. Indeed, great evils can follow when the Hebrew Bible is thought to bless an arrogantly inhumane nationalism, racism or legalism – and evils have followed in the history of many nations, including modern Israel. But even people who use the Bible to support such evils seldom live on the basis that all the 248 positive commandments and 365 prohibitions in the Law of Moses must be obeyed precisely. Disobedient children are not stoned to death. Interest on loans is thought normal. Most orthodox Jews accept the decision not to rebuild the temple in Jerusalem.

Almost all Christians have agreed that the Hebrew Bible was 'God-breathed and useful for teaching, rebuking, correcting and training in righteousness' (2 Timothy 3.16 in the New International Version) – which is why this constitutes about four-fifths of the Christian Bible, or five-sixths if the 'Apocrypha' are included. Without it, the New Testament is hard to understand and hard to connect with many realities (with politics, for example). But for Christians the Scriptures are intended to 'make you wise for salvation through faith in Christ Jesus' (verse 15) and many passages in the Hebrew Bible need correction in the light of Christ. To take only two examples, it cannot be true both that 'God is Love' and that he commanded the genocide of all the inhabitants of Canaan by the invading Hebrews (as when Deuteronomy 7.2 orders: 'you must exterminate them'). If 'Jesus is Lord', crucified during the Passover festival because God is Love, then God did not command that the blood of a lamb should be smeared on the door-posts so that he might know which house to 'pass over' while on his way to kill every first-born child or calf in Egypt (as in Exodus 12.21–30). And Christians have made such points – but not infallibly. The reinterpretation of the Hebrew Bible by the early Christians could be at the level of deep spiritual insight, but it could also and often not be based accurately on the original text or context of the passage. One explanation is that the text was often uncertain: in the Hebrew vowels were not added before AD 600 at the earliest, and the Greek translation could differ in many places from the Hebrew Bible, possibly because a different Hebrew text had been used. This, however, was the version of the Bible used by the writers of the New Testament.

There is nothing at all unlikely in the reports that Jesus quoted the Hebrew Bible with reverence and used it to understand and explain his own mission. The story of his temptations shows him balancing one passage against another in order to find the will of the Father, and when asked what the Father commanded most importantly he quoted Deuteronomy and Leviticus. And yet if he was always obedient to the Bible of his people, he and his followers would have been regarded by Jewish religious authorities as lying within the field of permitted debate, and his execution would have been blamed solely on the Roman colonial power – and there is no evidence that this attitude was ever taken.

The many Christians who in modern times have been convinced that the Bible must be rescued from fundamentalism, or from the appearance of it, have not been engaged in a conspiracy to gag God. On the contrary, their concern has been that Christian teachers who claim far too much about the Bible may discredit all their claims, and their own aim has been that God should be heard speaking through the Scriptures in the way he must have chosen if he has spoken at all through this medium. To such Christians – as to the educated public at large – it seems obvious that the Bible is not one book about which it might be reasonable to claim that it is the 'Word of God' word by word. If such a revelation had been intended, it would have been reasonable to expect the Creator of the universe to have been able and willing to inspire a written summary of the lessons learned about ancient Israel, a full and accurate account of the life of Jesus, a book of instructions agreed by the apostles, and a large work by Christianity's first and greatest theologian, Paul – or failing that, to inspire an official agreement about the contents of the Christian Bible before the fourth Christian century. So it seems that God chose otherwise.

In the Second Vatican Council the Roman Catholic bishops came dangerously near fundamentalism when they declared in their Dogmatic Constitution on the Divine Revelation that 'everything asserted by the inspired authors must be held to have been asserted by the Holy Spirit' – unless they meant only that when the authors were fully inspired they were right in their assertions. But all Christians would agree that the second half of this sentence was inspired: the Bible, the bishops said, 'must be acknowledged as teaching firmly, faithfully and without error the truth which God wanted put into the sacred writings *for the sake of our salvation*' (the italics are mine).

What is that truth?

*   *   *

John Stott calls the cross of Christ the 'heart of the gospel' and of course I am one of those who would very gladly agree (provided that the death is joined with the risen life), but I am also one of those who see no need to use the words 'propitiation' and 'expiation'. Not only do few people understand such words: when they are explained as meaning the payment of a penalty for wrongdoing and the appeasement of a person (these are the definitions in the *Oxford English Dictionary*), they seem to be unworthy.

The New Testament says repeatedly that Christ 'died for our sins' but 16 metaphors have been counted in a close study of how it communicates this understanding of the self-sacrifice on the cross. This is not surprising because although the sacrifices of animals were central to the religious practices of the time, among Jews and Gentiles alike, a clear and complete explanation of the system did not exist. The result was that devout people used the language of sacrifice unsystematically. We can see this if we turn to Isaiah 53, a meditation on the history of Israel which was (it seems) very much in the minds of Jesus and of the first Christians. There it is said very powerfully that all the peoples of the world have sinned but only Israel is despised, pain-wracked and stricken to death – and it is accepted that Israel's agony is necessary in God's purposes. Yet the Hebrew text does not make clear whether or not Israel is paying a penalty of punishment in order to appease God. It is said that 'the Lord laid on him the guilt of us all' and verse 10 can be translated as 'it was the Lord's will to crush him and make him suffer' (as in the New International Version). Yet the peoples of the world were wrong to consider him 'stricken by God' and verse 10 can be translated as 'the Lord took thought for his oppressed servant and healed him' (as in the Revised English Bible).

The same uncertainty about the right interpretation of a martyrdom can be seen in Christian teaching about the meaning of Christ's self-sacrifice.

The appeasement of the Father by the punishment of the Son was the standard teaching of the medieval Church and was reaffirmed by the Protestants in the age of the Reformation. In the Lutherans' Augsburg Confession (1530) Christ 'died in order to propitiate God's wrath'. In the Heidelberg Confession of the Reformed (or Calvinists) in 1563 'reparation for our sins could be made in no other way than through the death of the Son of God'. In the Articles of Religion to which the clergy of the Church of England subscribed in the period 1571–1975 Christ died 'to reconcile his Father to us, and to be a sacrifice, not only for original guilt, but also for all actual sins of men'. A twentieth-century reaffirmation may be found in the doctrinal basis of the Universities and Colleges Christian Fellowship. This insists that among 'the fundamental truths of Christianity' are:

1. the universal sinfulness and guilt of human nature since the fall, rendering man subject to God's wrath and condemnation;

2. redemption from the guilt, penalty and power of sin only through the sacrificial death once and for all time of our representative and substitute, Jesus Christ, the only mediator between God and man; and

3. justification as God's act of undeserved mercy, in which the sinner is pardoned of all his sins, and accepted as righteous in God's sight, only because of the righteousness of Christ imputed to him, this justification being received through faith alone.

A 'complementary' version of this basis has been authorized, but with changes in style rather than substance. One change is using the unisex plural instead of 'his' and 'him'. Others are adding the simpler words 'people are guilty' in (1), and in (3) saying that the righteousness of Christ is 'credited' to sinners and is 'to be received solely by trust in him'.

The word 'punishment' does not occur in that doctrinal basis but in her *Sacrifice and the Death of Christ* (1975) Frances Young observed that a common interpretation of the cross by Catholic and Protestant preachers has run something like this:

> God was angry with sinners. The Jews had tried to placate his anger by symbolically offering the lives of animals to him in place of their guilty selves. But this was inadequate and so Jesus offered a perfect sacrifice. He died as our substitute to appease God's anger.

This seems to be a fair summary of many sermons – and of hymns which have lodged the doctrine in people's minds, perhaps more effectively.

But there has been a large-scale reaction against that common interpretation of the cross. As I was reassured in our dialogue in *Essentials*, John Stott is among the leading Evangelicals who are fully aware that the killing of an animal as a religious act seems strange or offensive to modern people. Although he retains the language of temple-sacrifice because it is biblical he is also keenly sensitive to dangers involved in the use of this imagery. I quote his strong words because his teaching is likely to carry more weight than mine. He teaches that if Christ is pictured as 'intervening in order to pacify an angry God and wrest from him a grudging salvation', or if God is thought of as punishing 'the innocent Jesus in place of us the guilty sinners who had deserved the punishment', such presentations 'denigrate' the Father, who is then seen as a 'pitiless ogre'. He protests against any idea that God is 'subordinate to something outside and above himself which controls his actions, to which he is accountable, and from which he cannot free himself'. So 'any notion of penal substitution in which three independent actors play a role – the guilty party, the punitive judge and the innocent victim – is to be repudiated with the utmost vehemence'. There is in God 'no change of mind or heart secured by Christ' and 'it cannot be emphasized too strongly that God's love is the source, not the consequence, of the atonement'. So 'we are not to envisage him on a deck-chair, but on a cross. The God who allows us to suffer once suffered himself in Christ, and continues to suffer with us and for us today.'

I quoted Dr Stott's words with warm approval in my chapter in *Essentials* discussing his influential book on *The Cross of Christ* (1986). I do not wish to say merely that on the cross Christ is our teacher and example, for few sensitive Christians would nowadays think it adequate to say only that. Nor do I want to say merely that on the cross God becomes 'the fellow-sufferer who understands' (in A. N. Whitehead's famous words). I want to say that on the cross the darkness of the world has been overcome so that we can live in the light, for only if God forgives, only if he exercises his creative and sovereign power, only if he communicates his power so that people doomed by their own crimes and follies can break out of the trap, can there be a human prospect of ultimate victory. So I respectfully agree when Dr Stott teaches that God 'must satisfy both his justice and his love', if that means that God 'must be true to himself and not contradict himself', for God's character is 'holy love', which 'yearns over sinners while at the same time refusing to condone their sin'. But some disagreement remains, for Dr Stott has stood by his statement about the 'heart of the gospel' in *The Cross of Christ*: 'Evangelical Christians believe that in and through Christ crucified God substituted himself for us and bore our sins, dying in our place the death we deserved to die, in order that we might be restored to his favour and adopted into his family.'

Many Christians nowadays cannot accept some beliefs which lie in the background of that summary. To us it is not true that 'Jesus Christ, who had no need to die, died our death, the death our sins had deserved', for if he was human he was mortal. If the reference is to 'death' meaning exclusion from the life of God, I cannot believe with Dr Stott that on the cross 'an actual and dreadful separation took place between the Father and the Son'. A Father who deserted a Son who was dying in mental and physical agony because he had done that Father's will would find it hard to escape the charge of being a pitiless ogre retiring to a deck-chair in the wrong kind of self-satisfaction. Dr Stott says that the Father must 'appease his own righteous anger' but to me that is a very strange phrase, which again suggests behaviour which would seem wrong in any human parent. It seems simpler and truer to say that on the cross God was revealed, not appeased. God in Christ shared human suffering and death in order that we might see the extent of his unchanging love and be changed – changed not only by trusting in a righteousness which is 'imputed' to us while we are sinners but also, and chiefly, by letting ourselves be made righteous through a spiritual union with Christ and his Father.

If Dr Stott's summary of 'what Evangelical Christians believe' is the best interpretation of the cross as the 'heart of the gospel', it also seems very strange that it is difficult to find a parable which can communicate it to those who prefer stories to theories. In the 1990s the Alpha courses, Evangelical in origin, became popular as adult education or evangelism in the churches, and their chief communicator, Nicky Gumbel, wrote a widely used paperback, *Questions of Life* (1993). He avoided telling any parable which might suggest that God committed suicide in order to satisfy his own justice, but he did use a story about a judge who must impose a fine on a criminal but, having been a friend in schooldays, writes a cheque for the correct amount. No claim is made that any one parable is completely adequate but in this story some ideas which Dr Stott condemns seem to come flooding back: the law which inflexibly demands punishment, the judge who when the offender cannot offer anything sacrifices something less than himself, justice being satisfied when someone who is innocent pays the price, the emphasis on the satisfaction of a legal requirement rather than on reconciliation.

More appropriate parables were used by the Doctrine Commission of the Church of England in *The Mystery of Salvation* (1995). A mother playing chess with a child sees that the child is in a fix, not knowing how to move, but crosses over to the child's side and makes the best move before resuming the game. Or a pensioner whose home has been wrecked by vandals works with them to repair the damage. The commission was convinced that the idea that Jesus provided a sacrifice to appease an angry God had been virtually abandoned and that even 'the notion of God offering himself as a substitute to be punished for our sins is deeply repellent for many Christians today'. 'The twentieth century', it said, 'has seen a radical shift in our understanding of the nature of God', since 'a new emerging consensus has as its central conviction the solidarity of God in Christ with our sin and suffering' although these insights into God's own suffering 'have scarcely penetrated the official liturgies of the churches'. The commission also observed that 'over the last two centuries the decline in the churches of the western world of a belief in everlasting punishment has been one of the most notable transformations of Christian belief'. A sacrifice to God in order that we may be spared such punishment is, it seems, not needed. Instead we have 'God taking with the maximum seriousness our embodied condition' – by sharing our pains and our deaths.

If it is objected that the parables used by that commission do not take full account of the agony of the cross, we may compare the self-sacrifice of Jesus with actions which are readily understood in our time, as when a soldier or rescue worker loses his life in order to save others, or a 'prisoner of conscience' goes to jail in order that the people may have justice and freedom, or a nurse accepts great risks in order to help the helpless, or a mother accepts great sacrifices in order that a child may be born, fed and reared (Isaiah 42.14 represents God as saying 'now I groan like a woman in labour, panting and gasping'). The contrast between an act of heroism and a situation brought about by human evil will imply a condemnation of that evil, but the hero is a judge only in that sense and is not condemned in any sense at all. Death or imprisonment with torture may be the cost of heroism, and an infectious illness or labour pains may be the cost of nursing or birthing, but in no case is a penalty paid to a judge; the price is necessary because the situation is toughly demanding. Death may be what is expected by workers who enter a nuclear reactor in order to make it safe after a disaster, or by firefighters who enter a skyscraper already burning and about to collapse, and the world was moved by such heroism in Chernobyl or New York – but those people would have said that they were doing their jobs, in situations as unjust as could be imagined. To talk about the death of Jesus in connection with such sacrifices is not to trivialize the cross.

*   *   *

If it is objected that these comparisons with human heroes and heroines do not enter deeply enough into the mystery of a great act of God, it must be admitted that other comparisons used in the history of this doctrine did indeed go deeply. For centuries Christ's death was seen as the great ransom paid to Satan who had gained power over humankind, or (a little less mythologically) as the decisive victory over this power – and that meant much in the dark ages where devils seemed everywhere. Then the death was seen as the 'satisfaction' of God's honour (Anselm) or of his justice (Aquinas) – and that was full of meaning in a feudal society which depended on tenants 'satisfying' their superiors and on subjects keeping the 'king's peace' by behaving peaceably. But these interpretations have plainly lost their force.

If we seek a strong interpretation from the gospels, we find a situation which contrasts with any emphasis on the death as a legally necessary payment to Satan or the Father and as the supreme purpose of the whole life of the Saviour. Here not much is said to explain either the birth or the death and what is said says nothing about a need to appease God's wrath. In Mark's gospel (10.45) Jesus is willing to give his life as 'a ransom for many'; it is a reference to liberation from slavery. He also says (14.24) that his life's blood is 'poured out for many' because it is a sign of a new 'covenant' between God and the many; it is a reference to the practice of sacrificing an animal to mark a solemn agreement, as we might shake hands in public or share a meal.

Luke's gospel teaches that Messiah was 'bound to suffer in this way before entering upon his glory' and we read in the Acts of the Apostles that Jesus was given into the power of evil men 'by the deliberate will and plan of God' (Acts 2.33). But in the gospel's emphasis on the forgiveness of sins before the death of Jesus it is nowhere said that this depends on faith that the righteousness of the crucified Christ is imparted to humans whose sinfulness and guilt are universal. In the parables many people are sufficiently good to be compared with the Father, and Lazarus is said to be in heaven just because he had been poor; in the healings people are told simply to have faith in God; when Jesus is being hammered to the cross he prays for the forgiveness of his executioners on the ground that they do not know what they are doing; and the bandit is promised Paradise although it seems that he, too, does not know quite what he is doing when he speaks of his dying neighbour as a future king. According to Luke, the 'spirit of the Lord' was 'upon' Jesus not in order that he might die as a sacrifice to appease God's wrath but in order that he might proclaim 'the Lord's favour' (4.19).

In the fourth gospel the long speech to the disciples a few hours before the death teaches that 'the Son of Man is glorified and in him God is glorified' because Jesus brings knowledge of the Father and the power of the Spirit. Earlier it is said that the death will judge the world by showing the contrast between the light in it and the darkness in the world (3.19) but this death is meant not to 'judge the world' but to 'draw everyone' (12.31, 32). In this gospel the only sacrificial language comes in the acclamation of Jesus by the Baptist as 'the Lamb of God who takes away the sins of the world' (1.29), but no explanation is offered either there or in the brief reference in the First Letter of John to the atoning sacrifice for sin (2.2), in a passage which repeatedly stresses that 'God is love'. Clearly this gospel includes the belief that sins are forgiven but it seems significant that the actual word 'forgive' does not occur.

In the New Testament the Letter to Hebrews does expound Christ's sacrifice of himself as the 'sin-offering' by the high priest who has replaced all temple-sacrifices. Yet many biblical scholars have argued that this is not Paul's emphasis – indeed, not his clear teaching. He wrote in his second letter to the Corinthians that 'God was in Christ reconciling the world to himself, no longer holding people's misdeeds against them'. The Father achieved this reconciliation by placing the Son in whom his love was embodied alongside criminals, making him 'one with human sinfulness' in that sense but in order that 'we might become one with the righteousness of God' (5.19, 21). Thus Christ 'died for all' in order that through grateful love all might be reconciled to the Father – and 'see, everything has become new!' (5.15, 17). Christ's sacrificial death reveals what the 'justice' of God is: it is his way of righting wrong and that way demonstrates that he is truly 'just' and intends to have mercy on all (Romans 3.21–26, 11.32).

If Paul thought in terms of the sacrificial system familiar to his age – as he did, naturally – it seems necessary to attempt an interpretation of the cross which will speak with similar power to a modern world influenced by science. I now want to submit a suggestion that this may be possible if we start with what the fourth gospel does say: 'unless a grain of wheat falls into the ground and dies, it remains only that and nothing more; but if it dies, it bears a rich harvest' (12.24).

A colossal star had to die if the heavy chemical elements essential to the development of life were to be carried to Earth, and every cell in a living body has to die every six or seven years. Perhaps 500 million species had to die if there was to be room for the multitude of species now alive. Life has evolved through the superiority of the fortunate species in hunting and killing, and life has survived through the food-chain which dishes up other creatures. A sparrow has to fall if there is to be room and life for others and by the same principle we can understand why 'nature' allows three-quarters of all wild birds to die before breeding – and even why in fish and insects such losses are said to be about 999 in every thousand. And yet, if the Creator of each one of these creatures is both good and powerful, we do ask 'why?' When the sun shines we can be happy that it shines on good and bad alike but when people and animals die because there is no rain we ask 'why? why?' And when disappointments and tragedies pile up in human life we ask 'why? why? why?' No complete answer comes from the Bible or from anywhere else, but alone among the religions of the world Christianity claims that the Creator is expressed and embodied in a man whose life seemed to be a waste and whose death was an agony. So the cross may be a symbol of God's acceptance of many defeats because only thus can he achieve the victory he wants, the loving response of free humans – and that vision of God's cross may speak to a world where people may feel that they need to be forgiven but are more likely to feel that if God exists he needs to explain why so much evil has been permitted.

I noticed that Joel Edwards, the General Director of the Evangelical Alliance in Britain, in *The Cradle, the Cross and the Empty Tomb* (2000), taught that 'Jesus was paying the price for our sins' but added that 'it was *for some reason* the only way it could be done' (the italics are mine). Earlier he had questioned whether 'God' punished Jesus by forsaking him. Jesus, he wrote, 'actually became our bad stuff' so that 'no human sin existed in all the universe outside himself', but he asked: 'Would God go missing in his Son's most cruel and finest hour?' It would seem that this Evangelical leader found it simpler, and more convincing as an answer to human need, to preach that 'Jesus's cross was not just about *his* suffering. It was God's way of saying "I've been there".'

*   *   *

In response to another question which is extremely important, Dr Stott seems to me convincing. The question is whether it is necessary for us to believe that all those millions who die without ever having accepted Jesus Christ as 'Lord and Saviour' (in the terms understood by Evangelicals) will be condemned to the endless punishment of hell. Or is it better to agree with the Second Vatican Council? I quote from *Lumen Gentium*:

> Those also can attain to everlasting salvation who through no fault of their own do not know the gospel of Christ or his Church, yet sincerely seek God and, moved by grace, strive by their deeds to do his will as it is known to them through the dictates of conscience. Nor does divine Providence deny the help necessary for salvation to those who, without blame on their part, have not yet arrived at an explicit knowledge of God, but who strive to live a good life thanks to his grace. Whatever goodness or truth is found among them is looked upon by the Church as a preparation for the gospel.

Dr Stott made these straight replies to this question:

> I want to repudiate with all the vehemence of which I am capable the glibness, what almost appears to be the glee, with which some Evangelicals speak about hell . . . We both agree that the imagery which Jesus and his apostles used (the lake of fire, the outer darkness, the second death) is not meant to be interpreted literally.

After an exposition of all the relevant passages in the New Testament he wrote about the many which speak of the terrible and eternal reality of hell. But they do lead me to ask how God can in any meaningful sense be called 'everything to everybody' (1 Corinthians 15.28) while an unspecified number of people still continue in rebellion against him and under his judgement. It would be easier to hold together the awful reality of hell and the universal reign of God if hell means destruction and the impenitent are no more . . . I do not dogmatize about the position to which I have come. I hold it tentatively. But I do plead for frank dialogue among Evangelicals on the basis of Scripture. I also believe that the ultimate annihilation of the wicked should at least be accepted as a legitimate, biblically founded alternative to their eternal conscious torment.

Later he wrote that he is an 'agnostic' on the question of the possible ultimate salvation of non-Christians: he does not know, but he hopes. 'The fact is that God, alongside the most solemn warnings about our responsibility to respond to the gospel, has not revealed how he will deal with those who have never heard of it. We have to leave them in the hands of the God of infinite mercy and justice, who manifested those qualities most fully at the cross.' But he added: 'Like yourself, however, I am imbued with hope.'

I am left full of hope that the Evangelical movement will develop without insisting on the Bible being infallible or inerrant and on the interpretation of the cross as God's punishment. A wise Evangelical theologian, Donald Bloesch, has said that 'the ultimate, final authority is not Scripture but the living God as we find him in Jesus Christ' and in *The Future of Evangelical Christianity* (1983) he foresaw that 'the future belongs to that branch of Christendom that is willing to make itself expendable for the sake of the evangelization of the world to the greater glory of God'. I am moved and heartened by such courageous words, although I do not believe that the Evangelical movement would sacrifice itself, or its loyalty to the Bible's message, if it were to allow this faith as a legitimate alternative to older expressions. In *The Future of Christianity* (2002) Alister McGrath made the prediction that 'what is most likely to determine whether a Protestant congregation survives throughout the twenty-first century is not whether it is Anglican, Methodist or Presbyterian but whether it is evangelical or charismatic'. But the small e and c seem to be very significant, implying that the surviving Protestants may not need to belong to Evangelical or Charismatic organizations as they are at present, for all that is needed will be the essentials of Christianity. And in *Evangelicalism and the Future of Christianity* (1994) he listed these as the 'fundamental convictions':

1. The supreme authority of Scripture as a source of knowledge of God, and a guide to Christian living.
2. The majesty of Jesus Christ, both as incarnate God and Lord, and as the saviour of sinful humanity.
3. The lordship of the Holy Spirit.
4. The need for personal conversion.
5. The priority of evangelism for both individual Christians and the Church as a whole.
6. The importance of the Christian community for spiritual nourishment, fellowship and growth.

If these are the essentials, I am sure that a great multitude of Christians will join me in claiming that we, too, are evangelicals. Certainly they are what I believe. Certainly they must be strong in a vision of the Church that could be better than the Church of my lifetime in Britain.

CHAPTER 7

The Church That Could Be

H AVE THOSE HOPES been influenced too much by my own experiences, by the problems of church life in secularized Britain, and by modern Europe's reaction against its history as a continent dominated by churches? Certainly it seems right to base hope on experience and not on dreaming about the ideal, but it is equally certain that it would be wrong to attach the tremendous word 'Christian' to a church constructed merely to please one individual or one region of the world. So in this last chapter I try to place what seems essential in a setting very far from the scenes of my own life, from my country and from Europe.

In the autumn of 2001 I was able to see a little of China and to learn quite a lot from discussions about that vast and rapidly changing people, as a result of an invitation to talk and listen in St John's College in the University of Hong Kong. All the time I was asking myself whether the hopes in this book had any relevance to the future in China of the Gospel addressed to all nations, and I now offer brief notes about the relevance which I believe I have seen, connecting China with this little book chapter by chapter.

*   *   *

1. The book's starting point was the numerical decline of the European churches in the twentieth century. It is equally thought-provoking that Christian numbers in Asia are so small, approximately 3 per cent of the population. In China the numbers grew in the second half of the twentieth century, the Protestants from about 700,000 to perhaps 20 million, but even if those figures are accurate (and no one can know), and even if the Catholics, about 2,700,000 in 1949, now number 10 million (an optimistic figure), 30 million is not a numerical triumph in a population of about

1.3 billion: the triumph lies in survival. For half a century no foreign missionary has been allowed to work in China, no religious education for children has been permitted outside the home, there have been periods of harsh persecution and longer times of suspicion and humiliation, some Christian groups have become prisoners of conscience, the ruling Communist Party is still officially atheist – yet these Christians have survived and spread. But even now Christianity still seems curious to most of the Chinese. They do not forget how close in recent history were the links between the missionaries and the colonial powers. They do not feel that they have to explain why they are not Christians, any more than most Europeans have to explain why they are not Hindus.

Almost all observers argue that there is a spiritual vacuum in China today. The three 'high' religions prominent in its history, Confucianism, Daoism and Buddhism, seem to belong to history rather than the money-making present. Popular religion, to be seen in temples and homes, tended to merge all three religions but its power is now being eroded by the official treatment of much of it as a 'superstition', as not 'normal'. Already in the 1910s many members of the educated elite despised all religion. Since then the pressure of atheism has been such that in the 1990s the government could claim credit for tolerating 'religious believers' who, it reckoned, numbered altogether no more than 100 million out of the 1.3 billion (ignoring people who merely carried out the rituals and were not respected, and people classified as dangers to society and not tolerated). Yet Marxism as an ideology has also been discredited, by its brutality in suppressing all criticism, by the feuding and corruption of those in power, by the terrible cost of its crazy campaigns in economics, and finally by its own admission that capitalism makes more economic sense. Although in its early years Communism brought great benefits by ending the anarchy, by removing warlords and landlords, and by setting up basic health care, primary education and pensions, now the evil may be what is remembered. But if Christianity is to fill this spiritual vacuum, or (to be more realistically modest) if it is to have a major role in the future of China, evidently it will have to be shaped differently from what it was in the past (before 1950) and from what it is at present. And if it is too cautious, it may be banished to the history books, like Marxism.

So Europe and China are not so unlike, after all.

2. Another connection between Europe and China is, however, that many of the Chinese are still interested in spirituality and in morality based on spiritual insights. The development of Marxism into Maoism was in some sense a spiritual, even a religious, development: Mao Zedong's 'long march' in the 1930s was his time in the wilderness, he became the saviour of his people, his thoughts now constituted a holy book, his idealistic disciples were totally dedicated, processions and songs marked a pilgrimage into a new world under his banner, after his death he was treated as a god even when his policies had been abandoned. All this was in keeping with the very long and very rich history of Chinese religion and it is not surprising that after the collapse of Maoism there has been something of a religious revival, bringing some benefit to Christianity, more to Buddhism and most to family-centred popular religion in the villages where some 900 million people live. It seems that the Chinese do not need to be told that a renewed religion could have a role in filling the spiritual vacuum.

The great challenge to religion now comes not from Communist persecution but from science, for science is the essential foundation of the technology which is indispensable in the prosperous modernization which almost everyone now wants and which very large numbers are now beginning to welcome. And the traditional Chinese religions do not seem likely to survive strongly as modern education spreads the scientific worldview ever more widely, with the motto popular since 1978: 'seek truth from facts'.

Scholars rightly draw attention to many strong points in China's 'high' religions and to the emotional support provided by popular religion, but in all honesty it is hard to find an answer to current criticisms. For 25 centuries the Confucian tradition had strengthened the framework of Chinese society as emperors had come and gone, but as soon as China became a republic (in 1911) it was seen that modernization meant the abandonment of much of this tradition: its degree of reverence for ancestors amounted to stagnation and its degree of reverence for authority amounted to feudalism.

Buddhism has become China's main religion, but despite all its praise and practice of good works it has always remembered that its original message was one of escape from the suffering which comes along with life – escape by seeing that human existence is essentially not real but an illusion, not valuable but a disease to be cured. The problem as seen in Buddhism is that after death one is condemned to live many other lives, not necessarily in the same species, and thus to prolong one's suffering endlessly. The recommended solution is to blot out the self in *nirvana*, as a candle is blown out in the dark. The method is to lead a self-disciplined life and so to meditate that one ceases to be interested not only in ambition, greed or lust but also in life's life-giving hopes and fears, loves and hates, struggles and achievements. In China 'high' Buddhism has taken two main forms: Chan which is self-obliterating meditation not involving any divine help (transmitted to Japan as Zen), and Jingtu which, in contrast, relies on the faithful invocation of Amita Buddha so that the self may be admitted to the 'pure land' in eternity. Neither tradition seems likely to interact with the development of society.

Buddhism has interacted with China's native mystical tradition, Daoism: in another oversimple summary, this has become a search for peace of mind and immortality through a life in passive harmony with nature and through self-improvement through physical exercises. At a more popular level Buddhism has come to terms with the Chinese tradition of belief in many gods and spirits, all of whom can bestow benefits if petitioned by prayers and sacrifices. Stories have developed of the original Buddha preaching to the gods although actually he seems to have discouraged any interest in them. Buddhism has even accepted the practice of prayer to ancestors although its original message was that the ancestors either have ceased to be distinguishable as individuals or have taken new forms of life on earth. Strangest of all has been the encouragement in many Buddhist temples of fortune-telling, of materialistic prayers for a god's favour, and even of very down-to-earth ideas of what would benefit the dead (as in the burning of paper objects and money).

Many similar practices have been included in the history of Christianity, which is one reason why Christianity is now challenged along with the other religions by the triumph of modern science. But in China as elsewhere Christianity has had a substantial record of encouraging modern education and medicine, suggesting that it is ultimately compatible with science. It can be understood as a religion which stresses mystery but never seeks to be irrational; which marvels at nature but never deplores precise research into it and the determined use of it; which sees humanity as having origins in nature but also as being different from all other forms of evolved life; which believes in the one Creator rather than in control by many deities; which concentrates on the praise of God rather than on any kind of bargaining for blessings in return for sacrifices; which gives thanks for the continuous creativity of God but also for the freedom given by the Creator to the creation, and to humanity in particular; and which hopes for a share in eternal life, conceived as the life of God but neither as physical enjoyment nor as the total extinction of the self.

All the religions are challenged by modern knowledge, but in China as in Europe, Christianity may be able to offer the most convincing response.

3. Christianity's greatest asset is Christ, in whose human life God's own love takes a shape to which many are glad to surrender. He is an historical figure much of whose character and activity can be recovered from the evidence against the background of his own time in history – in contrast with Chinese deities who quite often seem to have originated in historical figures but who have developed through mythology out of recognition. But Christ walks out of history to make an overwhelming impact on disciples as the living Lord, with a personal appeal and power not matched by any other saviour. He can dominate an individual and fascinate a society, yet he is not an emperor in the objectionable styles of China's imperial dynasties or of Chairman Mao: he is humble to the extent of accepting death on a cross between bandits. Therefore people become martyrs out of love for him – and before death they live new lives because of him. The historical Jesus probably never knew that China existed, but the living Christ has been met on many roads, including the roads which cross China.

His message about government by God means liberation for poor and rich, for women and men, and for people of every race and nation, since it means that while rejoicing in the strength of his children God is on the side of the weak. That can inspire revolutions better than Mao's; it did inspire Sun Yat-sen, the Christian who was the first president of the Chinese republic in the 1910s. (Would that republic have survived and progressed if Japan had not invaded?) It is not a message which depends on mythology although myths have been added to it – or on metaphysics although speculations have also been added. It is a message that human life can rise to many joys on earth before rising to eternity. It is good news for China as for Europe.

4. If I glimpsed the 'kingdom of God' in the democracy of Trafalgar Square in the centre of London, where did I see it in China? I never went to Tiananmen Square in the centre of Beijing, polluted by the blood of the students shot down when protesting against a 'people's government' presiding over dictatorship and corruption. I had no wish to see the giant portrait of Mao, raised far above the people's heads as a modern idol. But I did walk among a cheerfully relaxed crowd by night along the Bund in Shanghai. They were admiring the floodlit buildings, historic or futuristic, on both sides of the great river, and the night was full of promise for a new day of social justice with peaceful prosperity, quite possibly with the world's largest economy. The central sculpture was a modernistic celebration of the coming of the Olympic Games to China. I happened to be there when China entered the World Trade Organization.

According to the message of Christ, government by God does not bring power to the clergy in alliance with the monarchy and the nobility. God's 'kingdom' is not like Tibet under the rule of monks and landlords, nor is it like the rule of emperors sanctified by the Neo-Confucianist religio-philosophy in China's equivalent to Europe's Middle Ages. A better clue to its character is provided by the secret societies which flourished despite the repression under the last of the imperial dynasties – societies which dreamed of a new China saved either by the Buddha of the Future (Maitreya) or by the Goddess of Compassion. Those societies resembled the people longing for deliverance by Messiah in the background to Jesus. They chose the way of violence, however, and the best clue to the character of the 'kingdom' which concerned Jesus is to be found in the current peaceful moves towards a genuine democracy and the rule of law in China, together with the growth of voluntary agencies which serve the people's needs without waiting for the government's decrees.

Many such projects have Buddhist sponsorship, now seeking a 'pure land' before death, but an excellent example is the social work connected with the Amity Foundation of the Protestant Christians. These projects are not anti-government, for people are by now profoundly aware that good governance is their greatest need and almost everyone hopes that Communism will be replaced without bloodshed – but they fill the gaps which, to be realistic, must be left by any government (and even now the government, seeing the gaps, sends some of its own social workers to be trained by the Anglican

Church in Hong Kong). The time has not come in China when it is wise for religious leaders or bodies to give the impression that they are 'interfering in politics' by public criticism of the government. Their silence says something to Christians in Europe who need both to understand such situations and to use far more actively their own freedom to speak to governments in critical solidarity. But Christians around the world may give thanks that even while China is still Communist the kingdom of God still grows.

5. When thinking about the Chinese churches today the most important hope and prayer has to be for their greater unity; at present Protestantism and Catholicism are officially classified by the government as two religions and they use different Chinese names for God. It is often thought that the most important hope and prayer ought to be for the churches' freedom, but in fact religious believers are given freedom by the constitution to worship and make themselves useful to society. All religious bodies have to register with the Religious Affairs Bureau at the national or local level and unavoidably some of the civil servants can be prejudiced against religion, but it is not a fair criticism to say that all religious leaders have to be stooges of the government. They have to be acceptable to the government but that proviso agrees with the main Christian tradition in the Church/State relationship, and the leaders are not openly appointed by the government as bishops still are in the Church of England.

When all foreign missionaries were expelled in 1949 many of the Christians continued to hope for the return of the Nationalist government which had fled in defeat to Taiwan and which survived on that island with American support. Quite soon, however, most of the Protestants in the mainland supported the Three-self Patriotic Movement whose policy was the acceptance of 'socialism' by churches committed to self-administration, self-support and self-propagation without foreign help. As an Anglican I cannot object to this policy: it was made the policy of the Church of England under Henry VIII in the 1530s. Nor can I condemn the Protestantism which emerged without the Anglican insistence on bishops, for many Anglicans accept non-episcopal churches founded in the rest of Europe as true churches. In the 1950s most of the Chinese Protestants, including Anglicans, were right to give priority to the need to be 'post-denominational' in order to end the accusation that being denominational meant being controlled, and encouraged to be divisive, from outside China. The subsequent growth has vindicated that judgement. Many courageous Protestants have persisted in belonging to 'underground' groups rather than to the officially registered congregations, but no voices have been raised for a return to denominationalism – which even in the West can be seen as an intrusion into the realities of our time from another country, the past.

However, an Anglican visiting China may feel more at home in the churches linked with the Patriotic Catholic Association, chiefly because there the Eucharist is the regular centre of worship. I felt that and my visit strengthened my conviction that the ultimate destiny of Anglicanism is to be poured into a reformed Catholicism. Indeed, in China it is already possible to see some of the shape of such a future. Already the worship of Catholics suggests that this kind of Christianity can appeal to many elements in the Chinese character. A Catholic church can be beautiful and mysterious, somewhat like a non-Christian temple; it can be adorned with art, it can use candles, incense, choral music and priestly robes; its sermons are not too long. But it also improves on the traditions of the temples; here a congregation participates, not merely watching the devotions of monks, and here a sacrifice is recalled but it is the sacrifice of Jesus, not the killing of an animal or the offering of fruit. Here the One God is worshipped through Christ in the power of the Spirit called Holy but the worship lifts the believer into the company of human saints including Mary who meets the Chinese instinct that the feminine (*yin*) is sacred. The worship also gives a sense of belonging to a spiritual fellowship which crosses the centuries and the continents – a sense of Catholicism being universal which need not involve the Chinese taking detailed instructions from Rome. And some of the problems which burden Catholics in the West have been solved pragmatically in China: to take two examples, here the philosophy of Plato and Aristotle is very little known, so that there is no tendency to teach Catholic doctrine in its language, and here parents who have more than one child are severely punished, so that there is no practical possibility of a religious ban on artificial contraception.

With these advantages, why has Catholicism grown far less than Protestantism since 1950? The answer is that severe handicaps have been imposed by the Vatican. (It is a repetition of the mistake made when the Jesuit mission which began in 1583 was making great progress by adopting Chinese customs, but was condemned by successive popes with the results that the mission collapsed and in 1724 any form of Christianity was declared illegal throughout the Chinese Empire.) In 2002 the Vatican has still not fully recognized the government of China; it persists in having diplomatic relations only with the so-called 'Republic of China' in Taiwan, and it persists in its right to appoint all bishops without allowing the choice to be made in China. It also persists in refusing to allow the marriage of diocesan priests although in China (as in Africa) there is by tradition little respect for an unmarried religious teacher who is not a monk. In practice most of the Chinese bishops have reached a private agreement with the Vatican, and some of the Chinese clergy have wives, but the shortage of priests is acute and unknown numbers of Catholics stay away from the 'patriotic' churches out of loyalty to the pope. The whole position of Rome has become uncertain: I heard a 'patriotic' priest preaching that the pope is infallible when he prays but not when he teaches. And where Rome is obeyed in defiance of the government, Catholicism has to be practised in secret.

In China as in Europe, the Vatican damages Catholicism by its present policies.

6. Therefore it still seems right for many Christians to protest against some forms taken by Catholicism, but it does not follow that a very conservative form of Evangelicalism or a very emotional form of Pentecostalism has a long-term future in China. At present the whole emphasis is rightly on preaching which explains the contents of the Bible and proclaims its central message: that is essential for the many new Christians who now look to the Protestant churches, and to the smaller 'meeting points' on weekdays, for instruction. But as modern education grows in China, 'critical' questions about the character and authority of the Bible are already beginning to revive debates between Christians which were active before the whole future of Christianity was called into question by the victory of Communism. For many Evangelicals outside China the move away from the defence of the Bible's 'infallibility' or 'entire truthfulness' has been eased by an emphasis on the Holy Spirit's gift of charismatic energy to people as well as to words, but here again China seems likely to raise questions. The Confucian tradition is still strong enough for 'clear intelligence' and emotional reserve to be admired, rather than ecstatic speech in 'tongues' not in any rational order. Spirit-filled 'prophecy' has to be distinguished sharply from the

spiritualist practices and the fortune-telling which are now illegal, as is healing through the exorcism of devils.

Such factors strengthen the possibility that many of the Chinese Protestants will sooner or later think that the message of the Bible is best communicated in a setting of reformed Catholicism, because in that setting can be found the strength of the sacraments, a wealth of spirituality and (at least potentially) a respect for all knowledge and all culture. And the heart of that biblical message is unlikely to be found in the idea that the just wrath of God against sinners needs to be satisfied by the sacrifice of Christ's death, for it has often been observed that in comparison with some other peoples the Chinese lack an acute sense of personal sinfulness. The idea that life ought to be lived in harmony with the decrees of 'the Lord on High' (*Shang Di*) or 'Heaven' (*Tian*) is both ancient and continuous in Chinese religion, but prayers and sacrifices have usually been thought to be needed to obtain blessings on people who are basically good (and often sinned against by the powerful), not for the sake of the appeasement of God by people whose hearts are thoroughly evil. On the other hand, the interpretation of Christ's self-sacrifice as the supreme instance of martyrdom in the cause of God's 'kingdom' connects with China's bitter experience that there is in humanity enough evil to demand extraordinary courage from the servants of God.

It therefore seems possible that in China, as in Britain or elsewhere in Europe, there could be a Church better able to communicate Christ's good news about God. There may be 'great Christian centuries to come' (a phrase used by Michael Ramsey). The numbers of churchgoers are now not large in comparison with the population – but the Christian Church was not large to begin with. It followed a Lord who was the announcer and embodiment of a 'kingdom' wider than any church, a visionary and a prophet who taught by telling stories, chiefly the story of his own life. And from that beginning came the most astonishing and most hopeful part of the world's history.

Index